BUSINESS FILING

Second Edition

BY

E. D. BASSETT

AND

PETER L. AGNEW

Published by

SOUTH-WESTERN PUBLISHING COMPANY

Cincinnati 27   Chicago 5   Dallas 2   Burlingame, Calif.   New Rochelle, N.Y.

E98

H861

Printed in the
United States of America

PREFACE

During the last decade, businessmen have become increasingly aware of the importance of filing to the successful functioning of business. Accordingly, they have recognized the need for better training of personnel in this field. Schools have responded to this need by including training for filing in their curriculums and by a widespread use of such training materials as BUSINESS FILING and FILING OFFICE PRACTICE.

BUSINESS FILING, Second Edition, includes all the fundamental material covered in the first edition. In addition, the textual matter and the illustrations are extended and improved to cover a much wider variety of information concerning the most modern systems and practices used in the filing of business records.

There is no standardized filing system that is best for all purposes. BUSINESS FILING, Second Edition, is therefore concerned with giving the filing student broad background training in filing principles and techniques. A student so trained should find no particular difficulty in understanding and using any filing system. While a number of the special filing systems are briefly considered, primary emphasis in BUSINESS FILING is given to those principles and techniques that are common to all systems of filing.

In BUSINESS FILING, Second Edition, the rules of alphabetic indexing are divided into related groups and are presented in logical sequence so that an understanding application of them is possible and the necessity for memorization is minimized. Card and correspondence filing methods are fully explained. The filing cycle is completed earlier in this new edition by presenting charge and follow-up methods and transfer methods immediately following the chapters on alphabetic filing. Numeric, subject, and geographic systems are then presented in separate chapters.

The practice set, FILING OFFICE PRACTICE, includes jobs for practice in filing under conditions comparable with those the student will encounter in a business office. To this end provision is made for practice in the most important phases of card filing and the most common systems of correspondence filing.

The authors deeply appreciate the cooperation of three very fine and competent consultants: Mrs. Alva R. Menzies, of A. R. Menzies Associates, filing consultants of New York; Miss Leta J. Stroben, formerly of the Globe-Wernicke Company and Record Controls, Inc. (filing consultants) and currently with the Record Planning Division of The Shaw-Walker Company; and Mr. Walter D. Mollison, systems consultant for the Schwabacher-Frey Company of San Francisco. In addition, the authors are indebted to the many users of the first edition of BUSINESS FILING who so generously gave suggestions for the improvement of the textbook.

ERNEST D. BASSETT
PETER L. AGNEW

CONTENTS

Chapter I

FILING—AND OFFICE RECORDS

Filing—Definition and Purpose *Filing* is the process of arranging and storing materials systematically so that they can be located easily when they are needed. Because a filing system provides a permanent and safe place for all materials related to the business affairs of a firm or an individual, the files are, in a sense, the "memory" of that firm or individual. Since it is impossible for any one person or group of persons to remember the details of all the events that have taken place during an extended period of time, the art of filing has been developed to perform this service and has become of great importance in modern business.

The main purposes of the various systems of filing are as follows:

1. To make records readily available when they are needed, whether for reference or evidence.
2. To keep all related materials together so that the history of the dealings with one firm or one individual will be available in one place. The materials may also be arranged so that those pertaining to one subject or one geographical area are grouped together.
3. To provide a permanent and safe place for records of business information and transactions during the time the records are not in use.

Files may also be used by business organizations to hold mailing and telephone lists, by clubs for membership lists and other records, and in the home for family accounts and recipes.

Filing Performed by Many Filing is performed by a wide variety of office workers. In small organizations, secretaries and stenographers usually do the filing. As the business grows larger, general clerks and typists supplement the staff of stenographers; and any or all of these office workers may and probably will do some filing.

Illustration 1A, A Central Filing Department

Large concerns usually have a central filing department in which special file clerks are employed under the direction of a filing supervisor.

Even in large firms where a special filing department is organized, however, a considerable amount of filing is done by secretaries, stenographers, typists, and clerks in separate files that are maintained by each department. One study indicates that 18 per cent of the working time of general clerical employees is devoted to filing.[1]

The Filing Job Whether employed full time as a file clerk or required to do filing as a part of some other office job, the person performing this task must have the following capacities.

---

[1] Potter, Thelma Maude, *An Analysis of the Work of General Clerical Employees.* (New York: Bureau of Publications, Teachers College, Columbia University), p. 86.

Knowledge of Alphabetic Sequences. All filing systems depend on alphabetic or numeric sequences, or on some combination of the two. Color is also an important element in some filing systems. Hence, an office worker who is to be effective in handling files must know alphabetic and numeric sequences, and for certain systems must not be color blind. The alphabetic sequence is by far the more important. Unfortunately, it is also the one with which many young people are unfamiliar. A knowledge of alphabetic sequence does not mean merely the capacity to recite the alphabet in correct sequence; it means being able to indicate what letter comes before or after any other letter without resorting to the long process of starting with a-b-c and reciting the whole alphabet (aloud or silently) until the letters in question are reached.

Reading Ability. A file clerk must be able to read quickly in order to understand the letter or other document to be filed. He must also be able to read details accurately, especially the names of people or firms to, from, or about which the letter or document is written.

Familiarity with Abbreviations. In order to be most efficient, the office worker engaged in filing must readily recognize the abbreviations of states and other geographic locations and know how to spell the names for which such abbreviations stand. He must also recognize easily the many common abbreviations that appear in correspondence. Such abbreviations can be found in any good reference book related to secretarial work.

Knowledge of the Rules for Alphabetizing. The rules for alphabetizing are presented in the next three chapters. They must be learned thoroughly, and no variations from them may be allowed to creep into practice. When either of two rules may be followed in a given situation, one of them must be adopted and then consistently followed. In large firms the filing supervisor usually establishes the set of rules to be followed in filing all records in that organization.

Personal Qualifications. Like all other office workers, the file clerk must have such personal qualities as honesty, good character, pleasing appearance, etc. A records clerk should possess certain other personal characteristics.

MANUAL DEXTERITY. Handling papers and cards requires a facility with the hands that some people possess to a high degree and others woefully lack. Cards must be arranged and rearranged; papers must be easily and quickly sorted, resorted, placed in folders, and otherwise handled. If you work easily with your hands, these activities present no problem; if your fingers are "all thumbs," your efficiency is likely to be low.

GOOD EYESIGHT. In order to read quickly and accurately, good eyesight or eyesight properly corrected by glasses is important. Every paper or card to be filed must be read in whole or in part, and it is vitally important that the reading be accurate.

MEMORY. A good memory is helpful on almost any job, but it is especially valuable in the file room. Office workers engaged in filing must unfailingly remember the rules. They also need to remember alphabetic sequences and numbers in some systems of filing and geographic locations in others.

ACCURACY. Accuracy also is a quality needed by all office workers, but it is especially important in a filing job. If correspondence is put in the wrong place, it may never be found; when someone wants it, it never helps the situation to say, "It must be somewhere." If correspondence cannot be produced when it is wanted, the system or the file clerk is at fault.

A good knowledge of filing is basic to practically every secretarial, stenographic, or clerical job in the office. Some office workers tolerate filing as a necessary but somewhat unpleasant phase of their jobs. Others accept it willingly, sometimes as a welcome relief from other duties. Still others find filing an almost fascinating experience; these are the ones that should make a career of it.

A person must be temperamentally suited to the work in order to be happy as a file clerk. The work is exacting; records must be filed accurately if they are to be located readily when called for. The work involves considerable reading and often results in eyestrain. The file clerk is shut away from most of the other office workers and away from customers, executives, and the other people who come in and out of an office. But there is a satisfaction in rendering a necessary and very valuable service to the business concern.

The Filing The filing department is a service department.
Supervisor The supervisor of the department must be familiar with all systems, equipment, and routines. She must keep up to date on all new developments in the records management field. She must train her clerks and develop in them the prime requisites of accuracy, neatness, and orderliness. She must impart enthusiasm and interest in this important function of a company's business. There are great opportunities in this field, and it is well for the student of filing to recognize the importance of the work and the opportunities it provides.

Scope of Filing The scope of filing is as broad as are the written records of modern business. Every written record that is of value should be filed. Among the many types of records that are commonly filed in business are the following:

1. All types of correspondence related to business matters —incoming letters, interoffice communications, telegrams, cablegrams, and carbon copies of outgoing communications.
2. Checks, statements, inventory lists, price lists, and statistical and accounting records.
3. Sales invoices, purchase orders, purchase requisitions, freight bills, bills of lading, shipping receipts.
4. Legal documents, which are invaluable records of business agreements and transactions.
5. Blueprints and maps.
6. Catalogs and trade magazines, which must be held in readiness for immediate use.
7. Newspaper and magazine clippings.
8. Records of stock, sales records, personnel records, library lists, and mailing lists.

Card Filing One of the simplest types of modern business files is the *alphabetic card file*. It consists of a file box or cabinet in which are kept in alphabetic order cards containing such information as the names and addresses of persons, businesses, and organizations.

The cards in a card file are usually white cards, 5 inches wide by 3 inches high (5" x 3"). They are ruled as shown in Illustration 1B so that the name to be filed may be written at the top for ease in filing and ready reference. The cards are placed in the file box so that these names are arranged in alphabetic order from front to back. Illustration 1D shows a drawer from a card file cabinet that contains cards of this kind.

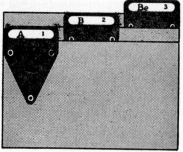

Aldridge, James (Dr.)

Dr. James Aldridge
1147 East Wedgewood Road
Tulsa 15, Oklahoma

Illustration 1B, File Card

Illustration 1C,
Card Guides with Metal Tabs

In order to facilitate the filing of the cards, and also the finding of them after they have been placed in the file drawer, partitions known as *guides* are used. These are special cards that divide the file drawer into convenient alphabetic sections as shown in Illustration 1C. These card guides are made of heavy cardboard or pressboard with projecting *tabs* on which printed *captions* indicate the alphabetic divisions into which the guides divide the cards. The tabs of guides are frequently one third the width of the guides; tabs of this width are described as *one-third-cut tabs*. They vary in position at the top of the guides so that they are staggered across the file drawer from left to right. In this way three different positions are provided. This staggering of positions enables the file clerk to read the captions more easily.

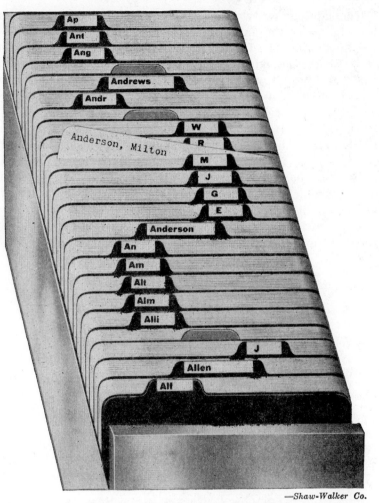

—*Shaw-Walker Co.*

Illustration 1D, Alphabetic Card File

In filing, cards are placed behind identifying guides. The captions on the guide tabs may consist of letters of the alphabet, or they may consist of names, as shown in Illustration 1D. Numbers are sometimes included in the captions to indicate the order for placing guides in the file drawer. (See Illustration 1C.)

The captions on two consecutive guides indicate the alphabetic range of the names to be filed between the two guides. In Illustration 1D, for example, the first guide is captioned *Alf*, and the second, *Allen*. Thus, cards bearing names from "Alf" to "Allen" would be filed between the first and second guides in this file drawer.

Need for   If cards in an alphabetic card file, or other **Filing Rules**   materials in other types of alphabetic files, are to be filed quickly and found easily, definite rules must be followed by the file clerk in determining the order in which the materials are to be filed. These rules are known as *rules for alphabetic indexing*. Everyone who uses a file must be so familiar with these rules that he can apply them in any filing situation.

QUESTIONS

1. What is filing?
2. Why are the files sometimes called the memory of a business?
3. Why are materials filed?
4. What are the purposes of a filing system?
5. Who does the filing (a) in a small office, (b) in a medium-size office, (c) in a large office?
6. What special abilities must the person who performs filing possess?
7. What personal qualities are most important to success in filing?
8. What are some of the advantages and disadvantages of being a file clerk?
9. What are the functions of a filing supervisor?
10. What types of materials other than letters are filed?
11. What is an alphabetic card file?
12. What is a guide? a caption? a one-third-cut tab?
13. What is the purpose of letter captions? of numbers used with letters as captions?
14. Why are filing rules necessary?

Chapter • 2

• RULES FOR ALPHABETIC INDEXING

The alphabetizing of names is the arranging of those names in A-to-Z sequence. It is the kind of arrangement that is used for names in a telephone directory and for words in a dictionary or an encyclopedia.

In an alphabetic arrangement, the name "Adams" is listed before "Baxter" because the first letters in the two names are different; "Baxter" is listed before "Becker" because the second letters in the two names are different. In other words, *the letter that determines the order of any two names in an alphabetic arrangement is the first letter that is different in the two names.*

The arrangement of names in proper order, however, is the simplest step in alphabetic filing. Two other preliminary steps cause most of the difficulty in alphabetic filing:

1. Determining the index order of the parts of each name; that is, the order in which the parts of the name of an individual, business, or organization should be considered. For example, the position of the names "John A. Doe" and "Henry A. Roe" in a file depends upon whether the first or last names are considered first. The surname is the most important part of the name and is therefore considered first in filing.
2. Determining what makes up each part of the name and how to consider each part in the filing arrangement. For example, the filing order of the two names "De Allis" and "Deal" depends upon whether the prefix "De" is considered as a separate unit of the name of an individual or is considered a part of the surname. Since in filing practice a surname prefix is considered a part of the surname, "Deal" comes before "De Allis."

The following rules for alphabetic indexing are concerned with such problems as those given above and constitute a guide for efficient alphabetic filing. These rules are divided into four groups: Group A, Names of Individuals; Group B, Business Names; Group C, Other Names; Group D, Cross Referencing.

Group A—Names of Individuals

1: Order of Indexing Units

Each part of the name of an individual is an indexing unit. For filing purposes the parts of an individual's name are considered in this order: (1) surname or last name, (2) first name, (3) middle name.

NOTE: In the examples that follow each rule, the names are arranged in correct alphabetic order.

Names	Index Order of Units		
	Unit 1	Unit 2	Unit 3
Henry Arthur Adams	Adams,	Henry	Arthur
Adam Neal Brown	Brown,	Adam	Neal
John Charles Herbert	Herbert,	John	Charles
James Hugh Wilson	Wilson,	James	Hugh
Kenneth Alan Wyatt	Wyatt,	Kenneth	Alan

2a: Surnames

When the surnames of individuals are different, the alphabetic order of those names is determined by the surnames alone.

Names	Names
Allen	Braun
Anders	Brown
Andersen	Browne
Anderson	Brownfield
Andrews	Browning
Andros	Bryson

NOTE 1: The letter that determines the alphabetic order of each surname in relationship to the preceding name in the list is underscored.

NOTE 2: "Anders" precedes "Andersen" because the "s" in "Anders" is not followed by any letter. This is an example of a rule that is sometimes stated as "Nothing precedes something."

2b: Surname Prefixes

A surname prefix is considered a part of the surname. These prefixes include D', Da, De, Del, Des, La, Mac, Mc, O', St., Van, Van der, Von, and Von der. Spacing between the prefix and the surname is of no significance.

Names	Index Order of Units	
	Unit 1	Unit 2
Leo Da Vinci	DaVinci,	Leo
John Dawson	Dawson,	John
Alice Des Laurier	DesLaurier,	Alice
George Macauley	Macauley,	George
Harry MacDonald	MacDonald,	Harry
Edward Mackenzie	Mackenzie,	Edward
Kate Madden	Madden,	Kate
Andrew McAuley	McAuley,	Andrew
Albert McDonald	McDonald,	Albert
Patrick O'Brien	O'Brien,	Patrick
Harold Ockrant	Ockrant,	Harold
Anna O'Connell	O'Connell,	Anna
Jeffrey O'Shea	O'Shea,	Jeffrey
Michael O'Sullivan	O'Sullivan,	Michael
Harry St. Clair	SaintClair,	Harry
Mary Vanatta	Vanatta,	Mary
John Van Buskirk	VanBuskirk,	John

2c: Compound Surnames

A compound surname (a surname containing a hyphen) is treated as one indexing unit.

Names	Index Order of Units	
	Unit 1	Unit 2
Mary Dean-Kite	Dean-Kite,	Mary
Alfred Grey-Mitchell	Grey-Mitchell,	Alfred
Pierre Mendes-France	Mendes-France,	Pierre
Frank Paul-Boncur	Paul-Boncur,	Frank
Helen Sinclair-Cowan	Sinclair-Cowan,	Helen

2d: Unusual Names

When it is difficult or impossible to decide which part of a name is the surname, the name of the individual should be indexed as it is written. (This type of name should be cross-referenced in the manner that is explained on page 31.)

Names	Index Order of Units	
	Unit 1	Unit 2
Kent Paul	Kent	Paul
Kodo Saike	Kodo	Saike
Kublai Khan	Kublai	Khan
Shaw Meade	Shaw	Meade
Wong Low	Wong	Low

3: First Names

When the surnames of individuals are alike, the alphabetic order is determined by first names.

Names	Index Order of Units	
	Unit 1	Unit 2
James Brown	Brown,	James
John Brown	Brown,	John

4: Middle Names

When the surnames and first names are alike, the alphabetic order is determined by the middle names.

Names	Index Order of Units		
	Unit 1	Unit 2	Unit 3
Larry Alvin Brown	Brown,	Larry	Alvin
Larry Keith Brown	Brown,	Larry	Keith

5: Initials and Abbreviations

An initial is considered as an indexing unit and precedes all names in the same unit beginning with the same letter as the initial. An abbreviated first or middle name or a nickname is considered as if it were written in full if the full name is known.

Names	Index Order of Units		
	Unit 1	Unit 2	Unit 3
D. A. Carlson	Carlson,	D.	A.
Daniel Carlson	Carlson,	Daniel	
Daniel R. Carlson	Carlson,	Daniel	R.
Daniel Robert Carlson	Carlson,	Daniel	Robert
J. E. Carlson	Carlson,	J.	E.
Jas. Carlson	Carlson,	James	
James E. Carlson	Carlson,	James	E.
S. P. Carlson	Carlson,	S.	P.
Samuel Carlson	Carlson,	Samuel	
Sam'l. J. Carlson	Carlson,	Samuel	J.
Sam O. Carlson	Carlson,	Samuel	O.

NOTE: The second and third names show another application of the rule "Nothing before something" because the second name has no middle initial or name, but in all other respects is identical with the third name.

6: Names of Married Women

If the legal name of a married woman (her given first name and maiden surname with her husband's surname, or her given first and middle names with her husband's surname), is known, it is used for filing purposes rather than her husband's name. "Mrs." is placed in parentheses at the end of the name but is not considered in filing. Her husband's name is given in parentheses below her legal name. (This type of name should be cross-referenced in the manner that is explained on page 31.)

Names	Index Order of Units		
	Unit 1	Unit 2	Unit 3
Mrs. Andrew C. (Mary Jones) Hill	Hill, (Mrs. Andrew C. Hill)	Mary	Jones (Mrs.)
Mrs. John A. (Anne Helen) Kramer	Kramer, (Mrs. John A. Kramer)	Anne	Helen (Mrs.)
Mrs. Harold J. (Mary Alice) Miller	Miller, (Mrs. Harold J. Miller)	Mary	Alice (Mrs.)

7: Titles

(A) A personal or professional title or degree usually is not considered in determining alphabetic order, but is written in parentheses at the end of the name for filing purposes.

(B) A title followed by a given name only is indexed as it is written.

Names	Index Order of Units	
	Unit 1	Unit 2
Father John	Father	John
Ralph Long, D. D.	Long,	Ralph (D. D.)
Dr. Vincent Macon	Macon,	Vincent (Dr.)
Professor George Mercer	Mercer,	George (Professor)
Miss Helen Meyer	Meyer,	Helen (Miss)
Sir Walter Raleigh	Raleigh	Walter (Sir)
Sister Ancilla	Sister	Ancilla

8: Seniority

A seniority designation, such as "Junior" and "Senior" or "II (Second)" and "III (Third)," is considered as an indexing unit at the end of the name.

Names	Index Order of Units		
	Unit 1	Unit 2	Unit 3
Edmond Williams, Jr.	Williams,	Edmond,	Junior
Edmond Williams, Sr.	Williams,	Edmond,	Senior
Walter Wilson	Wilson,	Walter	
Walter Wilson, II	Wilson,	Walter,	II
Walter Wilson, III	Wilson,	Walter,	III

9: Addresses

(A) When the full names of two or more individuals are identical, they are arranged according to the alphabetic order of the cities in the addresses. For this reason the word "City" should not be used in place of the city name in the address. (B) Names of states are not considered unless identical names of cities in different states are involved. (C) If the city and state names as well as the full names of the individuals are alike, the names are arranged according to the alphabetic order of the street names.*

Names	Index Order of Units		
	Unit 1	Unit 2	Unit 3
William Johnson, Boston	Johnson,	William,	Boston
William Johnson, Camden	Johnson,	William,	Camden
William Johnson, Duluth	Johnson,	William,	Duluth
James Smith, 23 Ivy Street, Boston 27	Order determined by street names, which are fifth indexing units in these examples (state is the fourth indexing unit)		
James Smith, 5216 June Street, Boston 4			

Typing File Cards   A file card usually includes the name of the individual in index form on the top line and the name and address in the customary envelope form below. In typing file cards, definite procedures should be followed. Type in the upper left-hand corner of the file card the surname of the individual, followed by the first name or initial, then by the middle name or initial. Separate the surname from the first name or initial with a comma.

Either capital letters or capital and lower case letters may be used. Some filing supervisors prefer to have the first index-

---

* If the street names are identical, the names are arranged according to the numeric order of the house numbers.

ing unit typed in all capital letters and the other indexing units typed in capital and lower case letters.

If the name contains a title, such as "Doctor," that is to be disregarded in filing, type the title in parentheses following the last indexing unit on the card. If the name includes a seniority designation, such as "Junior" and "Senior" or "II (Second)" and "III (Third)," however, type the seniority designation as a filing unit at the end of the name and separate it from the preceding unit with a comma.

Adams, John Eric		
Mr. John Eric Adams 2173 Western Avenue Duluth 5, Minnesota		

Illustration 2A, File Card
Correctly Typed

Adler, Ruth Esther (Mrs.)		
Adler, Henry J., III		
Adams, John Eric		
Adams, Chloe Ann (Mrs.) (Mrs. Brian J. Adams)		
Mrs. Chloe Ann Adams 2173 Wedgewood Road Duluth 15, Minnesota		

Illustration 2B, File Cards
Typed in Index Form

If the file card is to be filed according to a numeric system, the name is given a code number according to the rules of one of the numeric systems. The code number is then typed in the upper right-hand corner of the file card.

QUESTIONS

1. What is meant by the term "index order"?
2. In what order are the parts of a personal name considered for filing purposes?
3. Give your own example of the rule "Nothing precedes something."
4. What is a surname prefix?
5. What is the legal name of a married woman?

PROBLEMS

1. In each of the following names select the *first* indexing unit.

a. John A. Cramer
b. Helen Von der Hans
c. Sister Josephine
d. Walter Smith-Rudd

e. Mrs. Harold Fox
f. Wong Yie
g. Frank Martin, III
h. Peter McNamara

2. In each of the following names select the *second* indexing unit.

a. C. D. Weyand
b. Brother Emanuel
c. Lawrence C. Keenan
d. Percy Baden-Baden
e. R. Robert Adams

f. Mary Van de Vere
g. Mrs. J. R. (Corinne B.) King
h. Chas. Wentworth
i. David Gilmore, D. D.
j. William Jordan, Sr.

3. (a) Arrange each of the following names in correct index order on 5″ x 3″ index cards or slips of paper cut to that size. (b) Arrange the index cards in the order in which they would appear in a card file when filed correctly.

a. Will Howard Mackey
112 Monitor Avenue
Indianapolis 21, Indiana

b. William H. Mackie
414 Central Parkway
San Francisco 5, California

c. Willard J. MacDonald
171 Twain Avenue
Columbus 1, Ohio

d. W. H. McDonald
23 Elbron Avenue
Pittsburgh 12, Pennsylvania

e. Mrs. William H. Mackie
(Wilma H.)
678 River Road
Las Cruces, New Mexico

f. Willard J. MacDonald
221 Twain Avenue
Columbus 1, Ohio

g. William H. Mackey
4111 Glenway Avenue
Lexington, Kentucky

4. Is the order of the two names of persons in each of the following pairs correct or incorrect?

a. J. K. Hughes
   John C. Hughes
b. Marion O'Brien
   Oscar Obert
c. Donald Smith-Lund
   Mrs. Rose Smith Lund
d. Professor Carl Deters
   Carl Nathan Deters
e. Vernon Mayer, III
   Vernon Mayer, II

f. C. Donald Fuller
   Carl D. Fuller
g. Elsie Da Vinci
   Dan V. Simons
h. W. M. Finley
   Wm. Finley
i. Brother Joseph
   Ernest Brown
j. Al Bunker, Sr.
   Al Bunker, Jr.

5. The following twenty names are to be arranged in alphabetic order according to Steps A and B given below.

a. Dennis J. Paul *5*
b. Jerry Paul-Hansen
c. Mrs. Thomas J. Paulson *15*
   (Linda Sue)
d. D. Joseph Paulus
e. Harold Paul-Jones
f. Mary Ellen La Paul *1*
g. George Allan Paul
h. Dennis J. Paulus, Sr.
i. Brother Paul *5*
j. George Alvin Paul

k. Dr. Jeffrey W. Paulson *14*
l. Mrs. Walter T. La Paul
   (Marsha Lee)
m. D. James Paul *4*
n. Thos. J. Paulson *16*
o. Dennis J. Paulus, Jr.
p. Harry Paul-Herst *8*
q. Willard E. Paulsen *13*
r. George A. Paul
s. Robert St. Paul
t. Jeffrey Paulson, LL.B.

(A) Arrange each name in the order of its indexing units. For example:

	Unit 1	Unit 2	Unit 3	Unit 4
Dennis J. Paul	Paul,	Dennis	J.	

(B) Write the numbers 1 to 20 in sequence down the page. After No. 1 write the letter that represents the name that would appear first if these names were arranged in correct alphabetic sequence; after No. 2 write the letter that represents the name that would appear second, and so forth. For example, the first two answers would appear as follows:

1. (i)
2. (l)

6. The following ten names are to be arranged in alphabetic order according to Steps A and B given below.

a. Robert James Albert, Boston *4*
b. Wm. Alberts, Jr., New York *6*
c. Robert Kenneth D'Albert, Chicago *9*
d. Dr. Ralph P. Albertson, Los Angeles *7*
e. Stanley Albers, Columbus *2*
f. Sister Albert, Indianapolis *10*
g. Wm. Alberts, III, Lexington *5*
h. John Albert-Smith, Hartford *3*
i. Stanley Albers, Cincinnati *1*
j. Mrs. Walter R. Albertson, Louisville *8*
   (Wanda Lee)

(A) Arrange each name in the order of its indexing units.

(B) Write the numbers 1 to 10 in sequence down the page. After No. 1 write the letter that represents the name that would appear first if these names were arranged in correct alphabetic sequence; after No. 2 write the letter that represents the name that would appear second, and so forth.

Chapter · 3

RULES FOR ALPHABETIC INDEXING
(Continued)

Group B—Business Names

10: Order of Indexing Units

(A) The general rule is that the units of a firm name are considered in the order in which they are written. (B) When the firm name includes the name of an individual, however, the units in the individual name are considered in the same order as the units in a separate individual name.*

Names	Index Order of Units			
	Unit 1	Unit 2	Unit 3	Unit 4
Carlin, Merriam, Feely & Donohue	Carlin,	Merriam,	Feely (&)	Donohue
General Motors Corporation	General	Motors	Corporation	
Harry Karr, Charles Hall & Co.	Karr,	Harry,	Hall,	Charles
John Smith Dairy	Smith,	John,	Dairy	
Smith's Meat Market	Smith's	Meat	Market	
Southern Wholesale Grocery	Southern	Wholesale	Grocery	
Elmer Tyler Corporation	Tyler,	Elmer,	Corporation	
Williams Repair Shop	Williams	Repair	Shop	

11a: Units Considered in Filing

The indexing unit that determines alphabetic order is the first unit that is different in the names. When the first units of business names are identical, alphabetic order is determined by the second units. When both first and second units are identical, alphabetic order is determined by the third units in the business names.

---

* The names of second or third individuals in a firm name are considered in their transposed order.

Names	Index Order of Units			
	Unit 1	Unit 2	Unit 3	Unit 4
General Insurance Company	General	Insurance	Company	
General Textile Company	General	Textile	Company	
General Textile and Rubber Company	General	Textile	(and) Rubber	Company
General Tire & Supply Co.	General	Tire	(&) Supply	Company
General Tire and Tube Co.	General	Tire	(and) Tube	Company

11b: Words Disregarded

Articles (English), conjunctions, and prepositions are not considered as units for indexing purposes. They are usually enclosed in parentheses so that they will not be confused with the indexing units that are considered in filing. When the article "The" is the first word in a firm name, it is written in parentheses at the end of the name.

Names	Index Order of Units			
	Unit 1	Unit 2	Unit 3	Unit 4
Red and White Cab Company	Red (and)	White	Cab	Company
Red & White Stores	Red (&)	White	Stores	
The Red and White Stores of Ohio	Red (and)	White	Stores (of) Ohio	(The)
Red and White Stores in Utah	Red (and)	White	Stores (in) Utah	

12: Abbreviations

An abbreviation in a firm name, even though the abbreviation consists of a single letter, is considered as if it were written in full. If the word for which an abbreviation stands is unknown or cannot be ascertained, consider the abbreviation as a unit and index it as it is written.

Names	Index Order of Units		
	Unit 1	Unit 2	Unit 3
Culligan, Inc.	Culligan,	Incorporated	
Lawrence Electric Corp.	Lawrence	Electric	Corporation
Mt. Ranier Restaurant	Mount	Ranier	Restaurant
U. P. R. R.	Union	Pacific	Railroad
Warwick Co., Ltd.	Warwick	Company,	Limited
Zamora Cia., Sucs.	Zamora	Cia.,	Sucs.

13: Single Letters

A single letter in a firm name, other than an abbreviation, is considered as a separate filing unit and precedes all names in the same unit beginning with that same letter.

Names	Index Order of Units			
	Unit 1	Unit 2	Unit 3	Unit 4
ABC Mills	A	B	C	Mills
A-B Candy Company	A	B	Candy	Company
A to Z Stores	A (to)	Z	Stores	
J. A. Aarons & Son	Aarons,	J.	A. (&)	Son
C H B Products	C	H	B	Products
D & D Theater	D (&)	D	Theater	
Darwin & Jones	Darwin (&)	Jones		
E Z Wringer Dealers	E	Z	Wringer	Dealers

14: Numbers

A number in a business name is usually considered as being written out and is indexed as one unit.

Names	Index Order of Units		
	Unit 1	Unit 2	Unit 3
A 1 Meat Market	A	One	Meat
A & V Stores	A (&)	V	Stores
54th Avenue Store	Fifty-fourth	Avenue	Store
Grant and 22d Streets Bldg.	Grant (and)	Twenty-second	Streets
101 Swedish Delicacies	One hundred one	Swedish	Delicacies

NOTE: Although numbers are considered as words in indexing, they are usually written in figures in ordinary business usage.

15: Foreign Articles and Prefixes

A foreign article or prefix in a firm name is not a separate indexing unit, but is combined with the word that follows.

Names	Index Order of Units		
	Unit 1	Unit 2	Unit 3
D'Angeles Realty Co.	D'Angeles	Realty	Company
Du Barry Charm School	DuBarry	Charm	School
duBois Company, Inc.	duBois	Company,	Incorporated
Elbe Oil Company	Elbe	Oil	Company
El Rancho Inn	ElRancho	Inn	
La Belle Beauty Salon	LaBelle	Beauty	Salon
La Vogue Store	LaVogue	Store	
Le Grand Portrait Studio	LeGrand	Portrait	Studio
Van de Kamp Bakery	VandeKamp	Bakery	

16: Geographic Names

Each word in a geographic name, other than a foreign article or prefix, is a separate indexing unit.

Names	Index Order of Units		
	Unit 1	Unit 2	Unit 3
Ft. Worth Refinery	Fort	Worth	Refinery
Hudson Bay Trading Co.	Hudson	Bay	Trading
LaSalle Gift Shop	LaSalle	Gift	Shop
Los Angeles Tool Co.	LosAngeles	Tool	Company
New York News Service	New	York	News
Newport Evening Star	Newport	Evening	Star
Newtown Employment Bureau	Newtown	Employment	Bureau
Pt. Pleasant Box Co.	Point	Pleasant	Box
Portland Cement Co.	Portland	Cement	Company
Racine Wax Works	Racine	Wax	Works
St. Louis R. R.	Saint	Louis	Railroad
Salem Food Products	Salem	Food	Products
San Francisco Tailors	San	Francisco	Tailors
Santa Barbara Florists	Santa	Barbara	Florists

NOTE 1: The word "Saint" in a business name is indexed as a separate unit. Contrast this with the indexing of the word "Saint" in a surname. (Rule 2b.)

NOTE 2: Since the words "San" and "Santa" mean "Saint," they are not foreign articles or prefixes and are therefore indexed separately.

17: Hyphened Names and Words

(A) When two *words* or *names* in a firm name are combined with a hyphen, each is considered as a separate indexing unit. (B) A *single word* written with a hyphen is considered as one indexing unit. This rule also applies to a hyphened "coined" word in a firm name such as Al-N-Em Bakery.

Names	Index Order of Units		
	Unit 1	Unit 2	Unit 3
Addressograph-Multigraph Company	Addressograph	Multigraph	Company
Cuban-American Co.	Cuban	American	Company
Help-Ur-Self Laundry	Help-Ur-Self	Laundry	
Johns-Manville Co.	Johns	Manville	Company
Pre-eminent Brands, Incorporated	Pre-eminent	Brands,	Incorporated
Three-Way Medicine Company	Three	Way	Medicine

18: One Versus Two Units

When separate words in a business name (including points-
of-the-compass names such as *South West* in the name South
West Bank & Trust) are customarily written as one word,
these words are considered as one indexing unit.

Names	Index Order of Units		
	Unit 1	Unit 2	Unit 3
Goodwill Industries	Goodwill	Industries	
Good Will Products	GoodWill	Products	
Inter State Insurance Co.	InterState	Insurance	Company
North Western Lumber Company	NorthWestern	Lumber	Company
North-Western Supply Co.	NorthWestern	Supply	Company
Pan American Coffee Bureau	PanAmerican	Coffee	Bureau

19: Titles

A title in a firm name is a separate indexing unit and is
indexed in the order in which it appears in the name. (This
type of name should be cross-referenced in the manner that
is explained on page 30.)

Names	Index Order of Units		
	Unit 1	Unit 2	Unit 3
Dr. Sloan's Medicine	Doctor	Sloan's	Medicine
Laack & Williams	Laack (&)	Williams	
Madam Jeanne	Madam	Jeanne	
Madden and Powell	Madden (and)	Powell	
Mrs. Thomas' Candies	Mrs.	Thomas'	Candies

20: Possessives

When a possessive ends with "apostrophe s" ('s), the final
"s" is disregarded in that indexing unit. When the ending
is "s apostrophe" (s'), the final "s" is considered as a part
of the word.

Names	Index Order of Units		
	Unit 1	Unit 2	Unit 3
Boy's Life Magazine	Boy's	Life	Magazine
Boy Scouts of America	Boy	Scouts (of)	America
Boys' Clothing Store	Boys'	Clothing	Store
Morgan's Hardware Store	Morgan's	Hardware	Store
Morgans' Bakery	Morgans'	Bakery	
John Morgansan	Morgansan,	John	

21: Addresses

(A) When the names of two or more businesses in different cities are the same, the names are arranged alphabetically by names of cities. For this reason the word "City" should not be used in place of the city name in the address. (B) Names of states are not considered unless identical names of cities in different states are involved. (C) When a business has several branches located in the same city, the names are arranged alphabetically by streets. The name of the building in which the business is located should not be considered unless the name of the street is not provided.

Names	Index Order of Units			
	Unit 1	Unit 2	Unit 3	Unit 4
Desmond's, Beverly Hills	Desmond's,	Beverly	Hills	
Desmond's, Santa Monica	Desmond's,	Santa	Monica	
Hotel Supply Co., Atlanta	Hotel	Supply	Company,	Atlanta
Hotel Supply Co., Cleveland	Hotel	Supply	Company,	Cleveland
Hotel Supply Co., Denver	Hotel	Supply	Company,	Denver
Hotel Supply Co., Evanston	Hotel	Supply	Company,	Evanston
Lee Brothers Glenn Building 2302 Race Street	Lee	Brothers	Race	Street
Lee Brothers 1916 West Street	Lee	Brothers	West	Street
Lee Brothers Wirth Tower	Lee	Brothers	Wirth	Tower
Lee Brothers Young Building	Lee	Brothers	Young	Building

QUESTIONS

1. Is a geographic name that has a prefix considered a compound name?
2. Do the indexing rules for firm names distinguish between two words combined with a hyphen and a single word containing a hyphen?
3. Indicate the order of the indexing units in the name "John Henderson-Smith Co."
4. Why do you think that a distinction is made between words ending with "apostrophe s" and "s apostrophe"?

PROBLEMS

1. In each of the following names select the *first* indexing unit.

   a. 12th Avenue Hat Shop
   b. Blue Ridge Farms
   c. H. and R. Brown Store
   d. The George Hendricks Co.
   e. La Paloma Shirt Co.
   f. Southwest Dairies
   g. United Oil Products
   h. High Knob Coal Corp.
   i. XYZ Motor Service
   j. 177th and Elm Store

2. In each of the following names select the *second* indexing unit.

   a. South Eastern Tours, Inc.
   b. A. and D. Anderson Company
   c. Oliver-Johns Paper Co.
   d. La Crosse Insurance Co.
   e. St. Lawrence Steamship Co.
   f. Pre-eminent Candies, Inc.
   g. La Fille Shoppe
   h. New Haven News
   i. Harding's 208th Street Store
   j. Mrs. Todd's Cold Pills

3. (a) Arrange each of the following names in correct index order on 5″ x 3″ index cards or slips of paper cut to that size. (b) Arrange the index cards in the order in which they would appear in a card file when filed correctly.

   a. John Martin's Grocery Store
   b. J. Martins' TV Shop
   c. Marten Rug Company, Syracuse
   d. Marten Rug Company, Baltimore
   e. PFA Products
   f. P F and A Plumbers
   g. Mt. Lookout Novelty Shop
   h. Martin and 3d Avenue Shoppe
   i. El Matador School
   j. New Albany Insurance Company
   k. North Eastern Travel Agency
   l. North European Shipping Co.
   m. Mrs. Martin's Toiletries

4. Is the order of the two names of businesses in each of the
   following pairs correct or incorrect?

   a. Hadley Repair Shop
      Thomas Hadley Clothing Store
   b. Wm. Rawlings Supplies
      William Rawling's Supply Co.
   c. Moore and Hardy Company
      Moore-Hardy Corporation
   d. Mount Louise Gift Mart
      Mt. McKinley Hotel
   e. A to Z Sweet Mfrs.
      A-W Stores
   f. New Jersey Small Loan Co.
      Newburg Hotel
   g. La Mode Shoppe
      Lake Real Estate Company
   h. Jenkins'
      Jenkin's Tool Company
   i. Nurre and Drew
      Nurre-Anderson Company
   j. 10-Cent Store
      Adams' Dime Store

5. If the following names were written in correct alphabetic
   order, which name in each group would be *second* in order?

   a. Leo A. Harvey Store
      Harvey-Leonard Shoe Company
      Leonard A. Harvey
   b. Anderson's
      Andersen Machine Works
      Arnold Anderson
   c. Mrs. O. C. (Helen) Moran
      Helen Marie Moran
      Moran Hellen Corporation
   d. Bruce C. Nichols
      Nichols, Bruce, and Atlee, Inc.
      Bruce Carl Nichols
   e. Boy Scout Headquarters
      Boy's Coat Store
      Boys' Store
   f. B & D Meat Store
      B. D. Meader
      B. Donald Meader
   g. B. F. Food Store
      Better Brands, Inc.
      B. K. Biggers
   h. New York Cab Company
      H. L. Neufarth
      Newtown Steel Company

   (*This problem is completed on the next page.*)

i. Jones'
   Jones Rug Company
   Jones-Long Law Firm
j. La Vogue Shoppe
   Larimer-Adams, Inc.
   A. F. Larimer

JOB I—CARD FILING

*At this time complete Job 1 in FILING OFFICE PRAC-
TICE, Second Edition. The instructions and supplies for this
and the following jobs are included in the practice set.*

Chapter 4

RULES FOR ALPHABETIC INDEXING
(Concluded) and Cross Referencing

Group C—Other Names

22: Banks

(A) The city in which the bank is located is usually considered first, followed by the units in the name of the bank with the name of the state written last. (B) When the name of the city is the first part of the bank name, the name of the bank is considered first. (C) When most of the material that is filed is of a local nature or when material pertaining to banks is quite limited, the name of the bank may be considered first.

Names	Index Form
First National Bank Birmingham 5, Alabama	Birmingham: First National Bank, Alabama (5 units)
Cincinnati Savings Bank Cincinnati 2, Ohio	Cincinnati Savings Bank, Ohio (4 units)
Oak Ridge Savings Bank, Tennessee	Oak Ridge Savings Bank, Tennessee (5 units)
Farmers National Bank of Tulsa Tulsa 13, Oklahoma	Tulsa: Farmers National Bank, Oklahoma (5 units)
Central Trust Company Washington 26, D. C.	Washington: Central Trust Company, District (of) Columbia (6 units)

23: Names of Churches, Schools, Clubs, and Similar Organizations

The general rule for names of churches, schools, and other organizations is to index them as they are written.

A different index order is justified, however, when some word other than the first word in the name more clearly identifies the organization. For example, in the name First Congregational Church, the primary indexing unit would be *Congregational* rather than *First*.

27

Names	Index Form
American Legion	American Legion
Committee of Ten	Committee (of) Ten
First Congregational Church	Congregational Church, First
Roselawn Methodist Church	Methodist Church, Roselawn
St. Paul's Methodist Church	Methodist Church, St. Paul's
Loyal Order of Moose	Moose, Loyal Order (of)
Odd Fellows Lodge	Odd Fellows Lodge
Association of Retail Merchants	Retail Merchants, Association (of)
University of Wisconsin	Wisconsin, University (of)
University of Wyoming	Wyoming, University (of)

NOTE: When common usage is the basis for indexing, the head of the department should decide the order to be used.

24: Federal Government Offices

The parts of the name of a federal government office are considered in the following order: (a) United States Government (three indexing units), (b) the principal words in the name of the executive department, (c) the principal words in the name of the bureau, and (d) the principal words in the name of the division. Such words as "Department of," "Bureau of," and "Division of" are placed in parentheses and are disregarded for filing purposes.

Names	Index Form
Bureau of the Census	United States Government
U. S. Department of Commerce	Commerce (Department of)
	Census (Bureau of)
Division of Employment Statistics	United States Government
Bureau of Labor Statistics	Labor (Department of)
U. S. Department of Labor	Labor Statistics (Bureau of)
	Employment Statistics
	(Division of)

25: Names of Other Political Subdivisions

The parts of the name of an office in a state, county, city, or other political subdivision are considered in the following order: (a) the principal words in the name of the political subdivision, followed by its classification such as "State," "County," or "City," and (b) the principal word or words in the name of the department, board, or office.

Names	Index Form
Tax Collector Cook County, Illinois	Cook County (Illinois) Tax Collector
Iowa Civil Service Board	Iowa, State (of) Civil Service Board
Department of Public Works Seattle, Washington	Seattle, City (of), (Washington) Public Works (Department of)
Department of Public Welfare State of Washington	Washington, State (of) Public Welfare (Department of)

26: Foreign Governments

Agencies of foreign governments are indexed first under the name of the country, then subindexed by the principal words in the name of the division, bureau, commission, or board.

Natural Order	Index Form
Minister of Trade and Commerce, Canada	Canada: Trade (and) Commerce (Minister of)
Ministry of Agriculture, Great Britain	Great Britain: Agriculture (Ministry of)
Senate of Iran	Iran: Senate (of)
Federal Military Department, Switzerland	Switzerland: Military, Federal (Department)

27: Subjects

Certain materials are indexed by the subject to which they pertain rather than by the name of the individual, business, or organization. The reasons for this practice are: (a) Certain names may not be remembered and therefore could not be used for locating the materials after they had been filed. (b) Certain related materials involving different names need to be filed in one place. Work applications come under this rule since they are of primary value in relation to the subject concerned and the applicants' names are of secondary value.

Names	Index Form
Henry Meyer (Application for Employment)	Applications: Meyer, Henry
James Nordick (Application for Employment)	Applications: Nordick, James
Ray Poole (Bids on Equipment)	Bids (on) Equipment: Poole, Ray
L. S. Towne (Bids on Equipment)	Bids (on) Equipment: Towne, L. S.

Group D—Cross Referencing in Card Files

When names are properly indexed and arranged alphabetically in a card file, there is usually little difficulty in locating a card bearing a particular name. In some cases, however, difficulties are encountered because the unit in the name that was given first position for filing purposes is not considered as the first unit when an attempt to locate the card is made. In other instances the individual who seeks a card in the file thinks of a name that is secondary or that is similar in pronunciation or spelling to the one that served as a basis for the filing of the card.

Such difficulties are overcome in filing practice in one of two ways:

1. The index form of a name is used as a basis for filing the original card, and a second card is prepared for the same name in another form. This second card is called a *cross-reference card.*

2. The most important name on the original card is used for filing, and names of secondary importance that might be associated with the original name are used on cross-reference cards.

For example, *The National Magazine,* published by the Hopkins Publishing Company, may have been printed formerly under the name *The Interstate Weekly.* A new card prepared for a card file would probably bear the name "The National Magazine" and the date or approximate date the change was made, and two cross-reference cards might be prepared: one for the name of the publishing company and another for the former name of the magazine. This system makes it possible to locate the desired information easily and rapidly regardless of the name that first comes to mind, for each cross-reference card refers back to the original file card.

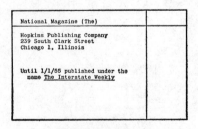

National Magazine (The)

Hopkins Publishing Company
239 South Clark Street
Chicago 1, Illinois

Until 1/1/55 published under the
name The Interstate Weekly

Illustration 4A,
Card for "The National Magazine"

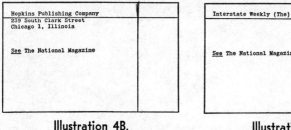

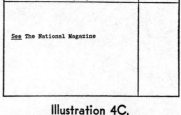

Illustration 4B, Card for the Hopkins Publishing Company as Cross Reference	**Illustration 4C,** Card for "The Interstate Weekly" as Cross Reference

The extent of cross referencing is determined by the needs of the office or business which the card file serves. If it is probable that more than one name will be associated with the same information or material, cross-reference cards should be used. The following rules illustrate the most common application of the principle of cross referencing.

28a: Unusual Individual Names

(See Rule 2d.) In cases where it is difficult to determine which is the given name and which is the surname, the first name is considered as the first filing unit on the original card and a cross-reference card is prepared, using the second name as the first filing unit, in the following form:

> Louhi, Kullervo
> See Kullervo Louhi
>
> Carter, Radford
> See Radford Carter

28b: Names of Married Women

(See Rule 6.) The husband's name should be used on the cross-reference card. For example, if the legal name of Mrs. Loretto Hill Johnson is written in index form on the original card, a cross-reference card for her name is written in the following form:

> Johnson, Howard T. (Mrs.)
> See Johnson, Loretto Hill (Mrs.)

28c: Similar Names

When several surnames are identical or similar in pronunciation but different in spelling, cross references should be made to each of the various spellings of the name as shown below.

```
Meier, see also Meyer, Meiers,
Meyers, Mires, Myers, Myres

Meyer, see also Meier, Meiers,
Meyers, Mires, Myers, Myres
```

28d: Combined Surnames in Firm Names

When a firm name includes two or more individual surnames, a cross-reference card should be prepared on the basis of each surname other than the first. For example, if an original card is made out for the Cornell-Harvey Novelty Store, a cross-reference card for the name is written in the following form:

```
Harvey
See Cornell-Harvey Novelty Store
```

If an original card is made out for the Smith, Dawson, and Orville Box Corporation, the two cross-reference cards would show the following information:

```
Dawson
See Smith, Dawson, and Orville Box Corporation

Orville
See Smith, Dawson, and Orville Box Corporation
```

28e: Initials and Abbreviations

(See Rules 12 and 13.) Many companies and associations, such as the National Office Management Association (NOMA), are referred to by initials. Cross references should be prepared for these abbreviated forms of the title.

```
BBA
See Batten, Barton & Avery

BBB
See Better Business Bureau
```

In the case of associations, it is usually best to cross-reference both the abbreviation of the title and the descriptive title.

AMA
See American Medical Association

Medical Association, American
See American Medical Association

QUESTIONS

1. In what respect is the rule for indexing the name of a bank different from rules for indexing the names of other organizations?
2. Would cards for the federal Departments of Agriculture and Defense be filed behind the same or different alphabetic guides?
3. Why should cards bearing the names of departments for New York City be filed in front of cards bearing the names of departments for the state of New York?
4. Give your own example of the use of a subject title in preference to the use of names of persons or businesses that are concerned.
5. What is a cross-reference card?
6. Give an example of a name that may need to be cross-indexed.

PROBLEMS

1. In each of the following names select the first indexing unit.
   a. Arizona Trust Company, Phoenix
   b. Central Bank, Los Angeles 12
   c. First National Bank, Spokane 4
   d. Farmers Savings & Loan Company, Springfield, Ohio
   e. Second National Bank, Galveston
   f. Savings and Trust Company, Washington 17, D. C.
   g. Colorado Savings Bank, Denver 9
   h. Federal Reserve Bank, Cleveland 20

2. In each of the following names select the first indexing unit.
   a. Veterans of Foreign Wars
   b. Knights of Columbus
   c. Iowa State College
   d. Rotary Club
   e. Association of Manufacturers
   f. R. S. Hillsdale Kindergarten
   g. University of Oregon
   h. Georgetown Alumni Club
   i. The Summit Country Day School
   j. St. Thomas Church

3. Indicate the order in which the parts of the following titles are considered in indexing. If a title is incomplete, add the necessary words to the title before indexing.

   a. Division of Cost Ascertainment
      Bureau of Accounts
      Post Office Department
      United States Government
   b. Bureau of the Mint
      Department of the Treasury
   c. Agriculture Conservation Programs Branch
      Production and Marketing Administration
      U. S. Department of Agriculture
   d. Federal Bureau of Investigation
      Department of Justice
      United States Government
   e. Bureau of Employment Compensation
      U. S. Department of Labor
   f. The Women's Army Corps
      U. S. Department of Defense

4. Indicate the order in which the parts of the following titles are considered in indexing.

   a. Department of Public Safety
      State of Alabama
   b. State Highway Patrol
      State of Iowa
   c. State Police
      New Mexico
   d. Park Commissioner
      Division of Parks
      California
   e. Civil Service Board
      State of Ohio
   f. Department of Public Works
      City of Baltimore
   g. Tax Collector
      Clermont County
   h. State Tax Collector
      Oregon

5. If the following names were written in correct alphabetic order, in what order would they appear?

   a. Tacoma Trust Company
      T-V Delicatessen
      T. W. Tacner
      Tennessee Valley Authority
   b. Ohio State University
      Old-Age Pension Board of Ohio
      Ohio Avenue Garage
      Ohio Potteries, Inc.
   c. Guardian Savings & Loan Co., Erie
      Waterworks Department of Erie
      E and R Restaurant
      George Erdley

    d. U. S. Federal Trade Commission
       United States Power Company
       Forty-Eight States Insurance Co.
       U. Samuel Powers
    e. Fulton Fish Market
       Federal Airways System
       First National Bank, Fort Thomas
       F & F Realtors
    f. Health Department of Cincinnati
       Library of Congress
       Columbus Memorial Library
       John L. Congress
    g. Department of National Defense, Canada
       Clarence E. Dawson
       University of Detroit
       Department of Public Works
    h. Mt. Carmel Hospital
       Mammoth Cave
       Monfort Stationery Supplies
       Highway Maintenance Division of Mt. Carmel

6. Each of the following groups of names contains three names in correct alphabetic order. A fourth name is given (underscored) below each group. Where in each group should the fourth name be placed?

    a. Johns'
       Johns' Gift Shop
       Johns Machine Company
       George John's Neighborhood Club
    b. A and D Garage
       Alice B. Manning
       Association of Manufacturers
       Allied Movers, Inc.
    c. Central Trust Company, Cairo
       Central Woolen Mfrs.
       Centre Theatre Guild
       Candy Kitchen
    d. Kiwanis Club of Hamilton
       Kwik-Freeze Ice Cream Co.
       J. H. Kyle
       Interstate Transport Company

7. In each of the following select (1) the name that would be used in preparing the original file card and (2) the name or names that would be used on cross-reference cards.

    a. Mrs. Walter A. (Mary Anne) Gibson
    b. Johnson, White and Carson Equipment Company
    c. The Corner Jewelry Shop, which is commonly called by the name Harry Adams' because of the popularity of the owner, Mr. Adams

JOBS 2 AND 3—CARD FILING AND CROSS REFERENCING

At this time complete Jobs 2 and 3 in FILING OFFICE PRACTICE, Second Edition. The instructions and supplies for these jobs are included in the practice set.

Chapter • 5

• ALPHABETIC CORRESPONDENCE
• FILES

General Nature of Correspondence Filing

Need for Cor- Every business finds it necessary to
respondence Files carry on a certain amount of correspondence. The volume of mail essential to the
operation of businesses varies from the hundreds of thousands
of communications received and sent out by a large mail-order
house to the relatively few pieces of correspondence that are
sufficient for the operation of a small retail store. Regardless
of the volume of mail handled by a business, however, a filing
system that will adequately take care of its correspondence
is needed. Probably 90 per cent of all correspondence filing
systems use the alphabetic arrangement because it is simple,
direct, and most readily understood by business workers.

Types of There are three general types of business
Correspondence correspondence: (a) incoming items, (b)
outgoing items, and (c) interoffice communications.

Incoming items consist of all papers—letters, telegrams,
purchase orders, invoices, statements, checks, reports—received by a firm through the mail or by messenger, or prepared from telephone conversations.

Outgoing items consist of all papers—letters, telegrams,
sales invoices, statements, checks—sent out by a firm to other
business concerns or to individuals through the mail or by
some other method of delivery. Outgoing materials are made
with one or more carbon or duplicated copies. The original
copies are mailed or delivered; the carbon copies, which are
often on colored paper, are retained by the sender and filed.

Interoffice communications consist of messages that are
sent to and received from the departments and branch offices
within a concern. Special forms are frequently used for communications of this type.

36

Olds, Penny & Gold, Inc.

Superior Paper Products

4138 Lake Street

Chicago

May 29, 19--

Mr. Winston T. Johnson
National Office Supply Company
214 New Britain Avenue
San Francisco 5, California

Dear Mr. Johnson:

Thank you very much for your order of May 28.
As you requested, we have sent the material to you
by express. Your invoice is enclosed.

If the shipment is not delivered within a
reasonable time, please let us know.

We appreciate your continued interest in our
products. We shall fill promptly all orders that
you send us.

Sincerely yours,

J. W. Van Horn

J. W. Van Horn, Manager

JWV:abc

Enclosure

Illustration 5A, Incoming Letter

June 2, 19--

Mr. James E. Chaney
Texas Cattle Growers Association
2143 Central Parkway
Austin 2, Texas

Dear Mr. Chaney

Thank you very much for writing us. The following
suggestions should solve the filing problems that
you described in your letter of May 31.

Since your tests involve much checking, probably of
similar data, we suggest that you use a solid file
cabinet and have 5" x 3" cards with names of the
most common types of cattle diseases printed down
one side. (See the illustration enclosed.) The
cards could be collected at the end of a test period
and filed behind subject guides. This would allow
you to keep all cards for future reference and investigation.

We are enclosing a cost estimate based on the data
you included in your letter of May 31.

If this plan seems feasible to you, let us know what
you wish printed on your tally cards and what subjects should be included in your file setup.

Sincerely yours

NATIONAL OFFICE SUPPLY COMPANY

Winston T. Johnson, Manager

jwr

Enclosures 2

Illustration 5B, Carbon Copy of an Outgoing Letter

Interoffice Communication

NATIONAL OFFICE SUPPLY COMPANY

112-118 S. W. FIRST AVENUE   PORTLAND 4, OREGON

Date: May 10, 19--

To: Winston T. Johnson, San Francisco, California

From: Walter D. Greenwood

Subject: Business Systems, Incorporated

Business Systems, Incorporated, is opening a branch office in San Francisco at 1300 Howard Street. The office manager will be Mr. J. Evan O'Connor.

This company is a good customer of ours in Portland and should give you preference for material to be purchased in San Francisco.

Mr. O'Connor plans to open the San Francisco office about the first of June.

Illustration 5C, Interoffice Communication

Purpose of Correspondence Filing   Incoming materials and carbon copies of outgoing materials that relate to the same company or subject are, in most instances, filed together so that the record of that company or subject will be complete. For example, when a purchase order is received from a customer, the purchase order, a carbon copy of the letter acknowledging the order, and a copy of the invoice covering the shipment are filed together. Thus a complete history of this particular transaction will be available in one place.

Interoffice communications are usually filed in a place separate from the general incoming and outgoing correspondence of the firm. Such memorandums or copies thereof are filed under the name of the individual, department, office, or subject to or about which they are written, or from which they were received.

39

Organization of an Alphabetic File

Vertical Filing Just as cards are filed vertically, that is, on edge, so is most correspondence filed. Vertical filing permits easy reference to an individual piece of correspondence and requires less space than if materials were piled one on top of the other in a flat, or "book type," file. To house correspondence vertically in alphabetic order, special filing equipment is used. This equipment commonly consists of one or more filing cabinets, each of which contains several drawers or compartments deep enough to permit the vertical filing of standard-sized letters or legal sheets.

Filing Cabinets Filing cabinets are made of wood or steel and have bin-type, sliding drawers that house filed materials. A correspondence file drawer contains folders, which are containers for correspondence, and guides, which serve the same purpose as guides in a card file.

Folders An alphabetic file *folder* is a container for correspondence. It is made of heavy paper that is folded across the width in such a way that the front part is approximately one-half inch shorter than the back part. An extra fold or crease is usually made about one-fourth inch from the bottom of the front part to allow for expansion in size.

Of the various types of folders made, the manila

Illustration 5D, Vertical Filing Cabinets

—Remington Rand

Illustration 5E, Folder

folder is the most commonly used in offices. Pressboard folders are heavier than manila folders and are used for manuscripts and other material that requires frequent handling.

At the top of the back part of the folder, there is usually a projection known as a *tab* on which the *caption* or title of the folder is written. A caption may be handwritten or typewritten directly on the tab or on a gummed label that is attached to the tab.

The tabs are frequently one fifth the width of the folders and for this reason such folders are described as *one-fifth cut.* Tabs are cut so that they appear in five different positions in the file drawer.

Folders are also made with tabs of other widths. Several of the most common types are: *straight-cut folders,* which have only one wide projection or tab which extends above the entire width of the front part of the folder; *one-half cut folders,* which have tabs, either at the right or the left of center, one half the width of the folder; and *one-third-cut folders,* with tabs at the right, the left, or the middle, one third the width of the entire folder.

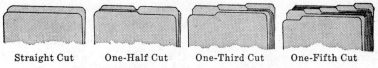

Straight Cut   One-Half Cut   One-Third Cut   One-Fifth Cut

Illustration 5F, Styles of Standard Tabbing

Folders are placed vertically in the file drawer with the fold at the bottom of the drawer and the open end (with the tab) standing upright so that a person looking at the drawer can read the tab captions at a glance.

Kinds of Folders Folders in alphabetic files can be classified as miscellaneous, special, and individual.

A *miscellaneous folder* is marked with an alphabetic caption, such as "B," and houses correspondence to, from, or about several companies or individuals with whom correspondence is not frequent and whose names have first indexing units that fall into the alphabetic range indicated by the caption on the folder.

A *special folder* holds material that relates to a particular subject, such as correspondence pertaining to a branch office or to applications for employment.

An *individual folder* is used for materials to, from, or about one company or one individual when such correspondence is active, regular, or important. Tabs on individual folders are often double the width of the tabs on other folders because more tab space is needed to record company names.

Guides A correspondence file, like a card file, includes guides. In general, guides serve two purposes:

1. They divide the file drawer into convenient sections so that the file clerk can locate a particular folder within a section easily.
2. Since guides are usually made of heavy pressboard, they help to keep material in the drawer from sagging.

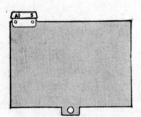

Guides are made with projecting tabs on which are printed captions indicating the sections into which the file drawer is divided. Captions are often in the form "A-Al 1" and "Am-Az 2." The combination of letters indicates the alphabetic range of the folders to be filed behind guides bearing such notations. The numbers indicate the order in which the guides are to be placed in the file drawer.

Illustration 5G,
Correspondence Guide

Kinds of Guides Those guides which show the principal alphabetic sections, in an alphabetic system are known as *primary guides*. The tabs of such guides usually appear in one or more of the first three positions.

Guides which indicate the location of materials of a special nature, such as correspondence pertaining to applications, are known as *auxiliary* or *special guides*. They are used to speed filing and finding by calling attention to the more important subsections.

Arrangement of Guides and Folders There are many possible arrangements of the different types of guides and folders in an alphabetic correspondence file. One general principle, however, applies to all arrange-

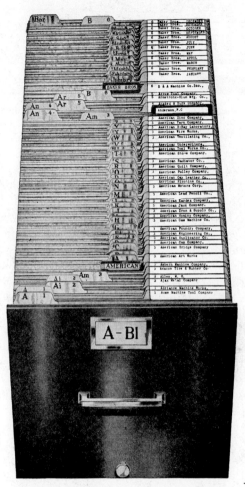

—*Globe-Wernicke*

Illustration 5H,
Drawer of an Alphabetic File

ments. *A primary guide always precedes all other material in a section, including special guides, special folders, individual folders, and miscellaneous folders, that fall within the range covered by that primary guide.* The following is a description of an arrangement illustrated on page 44.

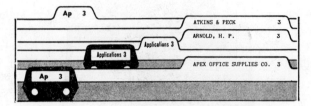

Illustration 51, One Arrangement of Guides
and Folders

Assume that the correspondence carried on by a certain
company is of such a volume that it is necessary to divide
the file into more sections than would be possible by using
single letters of the alphabet, and that the "A" folders are
grouped into three sections—A 1, Al 2, and Ap 3. These three
sections are indicated on primary guides in first position.
A description of the Ap-3 section will indicate the general
nature of the system.

The first item in the Ap-3 section is the primary guide
labeled "Ap 3." This guide is in first position and introduces
folders which hold correspondence from, to, or about companies, individuals, and subjects that have first indexing
units beginning with the letters Ap to Az. Note that the number "3" is recorded on the guide tab. This number indicates
the section of the file in which the guide is located.

The second item in the Ap-3 section is an individual folder
for the Apex Office Supplies Company. This folder was
opened because the correspondence with the Apex Office Supplies Company was active and regular. The individual folder
is in fifth position.

The third item in the Ap-3 section is a special guide labeled
"Applications." Applications for employment, which are
received at rather frequent intervals, must be filed in one
special place so that they will be available as a group. For
this reason a folder for applications is used. The special
guide that indicates the position of the special folder for
these communications is in third position. It follows immediately after the individual folder for the Apex Office Supplies
Company because "Applications" falls alphabetically after
"Apex."

The fourth item in the Ap-3 section, then, is the special folder labeled "Applications." In this folder is placed all the correspondence relating to this subject. Since it represents a special division of the Ap-3 section, it is placed in a position reserved for special divisions. This position is fourth position.

The fifth item in the Ap-3 section is an individual folder for H. P. Arnold. This folder was opened because the correspondence with Mr. Arnold was active and regular. The folder is in fifth position. It falls immediately after the special Applications folder because "Arnold" follows "Applications" in an alphabetic arrangement.

The sixth item in the Ap-3 section is an individual folder for Atkins & Peck. This folder, like those for the Apex Office Supplies Company and H. P. Arnold, was opened because the correspondence with this firm was active and regular. The folder is also in fifth position, and is placed immediately after the H. P. Arnold folder because "Atkins" falls alphabetically after "Arnold."

The seventh item in the Ap-3 section is a miscellaneous folder in second position labeled "Ap 3." This folder contains all the correspondence with firms and individuals whose names begin with Ap to Az and whose correspondence is not filed either in a special folder or in an individual folder. Since it is a miscellaneous folder, this folder is placed last in the section.

The following summary of this filing system indicates the purpose of each position.

First Position:
> For primary guides, which indicate the alphabetic sections into which the filing system is divided.

Second Position:
> For miscellaneous folders, which bear the same captions as the primary guides and which house all the correspondence with individuals or companies for whom no special folder in fourth position or individual folder in fifth position is provided.

Third Position:
> For special guides, which indicate the placement of special folders.

Fourth Position:
For special folders, such as those which are opened to
take care of letters pertaining to the same type of subject
matter. Letters concerned with applications are usually
filed in a folder of this type.
Fifth Position:
For individual folders, which are added to the file when
correspondence with one individual or company accumu-
lates to a number of pieces that warrants the opening
of such a folder.

Special Sections

Kinds of   There are three main types of special sec-
Special Sections tions that are used in alphabetic filing
                      systems: special subject sections, special
name or title sections, and special date sections.

Special Subject   Special subject sections are often included
Sections   in alphabetic filing systems as an aid to
                      efficient filing. A special subject guide and
a special subject folder should be added if it is found that any
particular phase of a business is important enough to warrant
the filing of correspondence in relation to that subject. "Applications" (for employment) constitutes an example of the
subject sections for which provision is often made.

Time and money can be saved by grouping material so that
all related data can be filed rapidly and found easily, and the
adding of a special subject section may greatly increase the
efficiency of a filing system. As a consequence, the efficiency
of an entire business organization may be improved.

A special subject section is similar in appearance to a
special name section. (See Illustration 5J.)

Special Name or   This type of special section can be very
Title Sections   advantageous when added to an alphabetic
                      file. A common name such as Brown,
Smith, or Jones brings masses of material into one section of
an alphabetic file and so overcrowds the miscellaneous folder
for that section that efficient filing is impossible. If a special

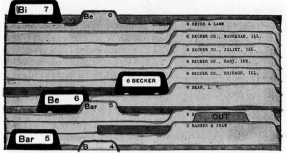

—*Automatic File & Index Co.*

Illustration 5J, File Section with Special Name Guide

guide and a special folder are added for each name that is repeated a large number of times, the congestion in the file will be lessened. For example, if a filing system is crowded with material concerning the name "Smith," a special guide labeled "Smith" and a special folder labeled "Smith" will prove useful. All the miscellaneous correspondence with individuals or firms by the name of "Smith" can be housed in the one folder, and the file will be easier to use. Furthermore, the special Smith guide serves to locate all individual folders for names that have Smith as the first indexing unit.

In Illustration 5J a special guide labeled "Becker" used to mark the location of all individual folders for names that have Becker as the first indexing unit.

Another example of the need for a special guide and a special miscellaneous folder is that in which a number of firm names begin with the name of a city, such as New York Hat Store, New York Iron Works, and New York Stores, Inc.

If there are so many correspondents with similar names that one special folder would contain too much material, a number of special folders could be used behind the special guide. These would be labeled with the name of the guide and the division of the alphabet covered by the folder. For example, the "Smith" guide could be followed by special folders with notations "Smith A-D," "Smith E-H," "Smith I-L," and so on. These folders would break down the Smith section into smaller groups according to the second filing unit. The same principle could be applied to names such as New York.

Special Date Sections   Date sections are commonly used when one individual folder is not adequate for the amount of material received for filing. For example, a date section may consist of four folders, one for each quarter of the year. The inclusive dates should appear on each folder, as:

1955
Jan.-March

BECKER COMPANY

QUESTIONS

1. Why does every business need some type of correspondence filing system?
2. What are the three general types of business correspondence?
3. Of what kinds of papers does each type of business correspondence consist?
4. What is the purpose of correspondence filing?
5. What is meant by the term "vertical filing"?
6. What are the advantages of vertical filing?
7. What is a filing cabinet?
8. For what purpose is a folder used?
9. Describe a folder.
10. What is the difference between a tab and a caption on a folder?
11. What does the expression "one-fifth-cut folder" mean?
12. In filing, to what does the term "position" refer?
13. What is a straight-cut folder? a one-half-cut folder? a one-third-cut folder?
14. How is a folder placed in a file drawer for vertical filing?
15. What is a miscellaneous folder? a special folder? an individual folder?
16. For what purposes are guides used in a correspondence file?
17. What is a primary guide? an auxiliary guide?
18. Describe the arrangement of guides and folders that is illustrated on page 44.
19. What are the three main types of special sections used in alphabetic filing systems? Describe each type.

PROBLEMS

1. A file drawer contains primary guides in first position, miscellaneous folders in second position, and individual folders in fifth position. A special folder for companies with names beginning with the word "American" and a special guide to indicate the location of this special folder and of several individual folders for companies whose names begin with "American" are to be added. In what positions would these two new items be placed?

2. A file drawer contains primary guides in first position labeled "A 1," "B 2," "Bi 3," and "Br 4"; corresponding miscellaneous folders in second position; and individual folders in fifth position. The file clerk has been instructed by the office manager to organize the correspondence file in such a manner that all correspondence with banks will be located in consecutive folders in one section of the file. Behind which guide and in what positions should these additional items be placed?

3. In the first file drawer of a filing cabinet there are:
   a. five primary guides in first position labeled "A 1," "Am 2," "B 3," "Be 4," and "Br 5."
   b. two auxiliary guides in third position labeled "Applications 2" and "Branch Office 5."
   c. five miscellaneous folders in second position with labels corresponding to the notations on the tabs of the primary guides.
   d. two special folders in fourth position with labels corresponding to the notations on the tabs of the auxiliary guides.
   e. six individual folders in fifth position with the following labels: "Abrams Novelty Store"; "American Toy Mfg. Co."; "Atlas Department Store"; "Bay View Antique Shoppe"; "Brown Doll Company"; "Brown, Frank."

   Indicate the order, item by item from front to back, in which these supplies are placed in the file drawer.

4. The Br section of a file drawer contains the following items: a primary Br guide, a miscellaneous Br folder, an auxiliary Brown guide, a special Brown folder, and several individual folders for individuals and businesses with names that have "Brown" as the first filing unit. Indicate the kind of folder in which each of the following communications would be filed.
   a. A letter from Wallace R. Brown, with whom the business has infrequent correspondence.

(This problem is completed on the next page.)

b. The carbon of a letter to A. J. Braun, with whom the business has infrequent correspondence.

c. A telegram from Brown, Jackson, and Yates, with whom the business has frequent correspondence.

d. The carbon of a letter to the Browning Garage, with which the business has infrequent correspondence.

5. In a file drawer of a filing cabinet there are:

a. five primary guides in first position labeled "R 1," "Re 2," "Ro 3," "S 4," and "St 5."

b. two auxiliary guides in third position labeled "Receiving Office 2" and "Southside Branch 4."

c. five miscellaneous folders in second position with labels corresponding to the notations on the tabs of the primary guides.

d. two special folders in fourth position with labels corresponding to the notations on the tabs of the auxiliary guides.

e. six individual folders in fifth position with the following labels: "Raymond Department Store," "Regional Supply Co.," "Rollman's Coffee Shop," "Smedley, Joseph," "Strietmann Repair Shop," and "Strauss Music Store."

Indicate the order, item by item from front to back, in which these supplies are placed in the file drawer.

Chapter 6

• ALPHABETIC CORRESPONDENCE
• FILING PROCEDURE

Procedures Preliminary to Filing

When incoming correspondence reaches the filing department, it usually bears two stamps or marks—a time stamp and a release mark. The file clerk must know the nature and significance of both marks.

Time Stamp When incoming mail is received, the mail clerk opens it and stamps each piece of correspondence with a rubber stamp or a machine in order to mark the date and the time the letter was opened. This mark is known as a *time stamp*. It serves as a record of the time that the letter was received by the company and helps to fix responsibility for the lapse of time before the letter is answered. (See Illustration 6A, page 52.)

Release Mark After the mail is stamped by the mail clerk, it is sorted according to individuals or departments and is delivered to the proper persons for attention. The person to whom the letter is addressed (addressee), or someone appointed by him, answers the letter. After the secretary has typed the reply, she sends the two pieces of correspondence (the incoming original and the carbon copy of the reply) to the filing department for filing. Before the secretary sends the original letter, however, she marks her initials in the upper left-hand corner to indicate to the file clerk that the letter has been released by her to be filed. The initials of the secretary or those of her employer, or other mark if a rubber stamp is used, are known as a *release mark* ("D. A." in Illustration 6A.) The release mark gives the file clerk the authority to file the letter.

It is not necessary to place a release mark on the carbon copy of an outgoing letter because the file clerk may always assume that a carbon copy sent to the filing department is ready to be filed.

CALIFORNIA BUILDING MATERIALS COMPANY

4582 Wilshire Boulevard

LOS ANGELES 14, CALIFORNIA

D.l.

May 10, 19--

MAY 12 9 16 AM 19--

Mr. Winston T. Johnson
National Office Supply Company
214 New Britain Avenue
San Francisco 5, California

Dear Mr. Johnson

       There will be a Building Materials
Dealers Convention June 30 to July 2 at the
Civic Auditorium, Los Angeles. We should like
to have you as our speaker at a luncheon meet-
ing July 1, at 12:15, at the Biltmore Hotel.

       Since you have made a study of social
security records, we know that you could give
us some good ideas along this line.

       Please let me know soon if you will
be available for this date.

           Very truly yours

           J. F. Fenton

           J. F. Fenton, Secretary

RD

**Illustration 6A, Incoming Letter Showing a Letterhead, a Time Stamp,
and a Release Mark**

Filing Procedure

Inspection The first responsibility of the file clerk is to inspect each incoming letter to see that it has been released for filing. This type of inspection is not necessary, of course, for carbon copies of outgoing letters.

Rules for Coding Correspondence that is sent to the filing department may be marked to indicate its proper placement in the file. If it is not marked in this manner, the file clerk reads it to see whether it contains anything that has a bearing on its placement in the file. She then marks the letter in such a way that the folder in which it should be placed is indicated. The marking of a letter for this purpose is known as *coding*.

In general, correspondence is filed under the most important name appearing on it because that is the name most likely to be used in referring to that piece of material or in calling for it from the files. It is necessary for the file clerk to be familiar with definite rules, however, if she is to be able to determine which of several names that may appear in one letter is the most important for filing purposes.

The following rules apply to the coding of correspondence.

1. The name of the business firm is usually coded when:
   a. That name is a part of the letterhead of an incoming letter.
   b. That name appears in the heading or as a part of the signature when the letter is written on plain paper.
   c. That name is used in the inside address of an outgoing letter.
   d. That name is mentioned in the body of the letter and is the most important name in the letter.

2. When the name of the business is known but does not appear on an incoming communication signed by an individual, the company name rather than the individual's name should be used as the basis for coding. If an incoming business letter from John Jones does not refer to or bear the name of the business that he represents, the letter would be coded with the name of the writer and filed in a miscellaneous folder. Later if the name of his business is learned, the correspondence should be transferred to the proper miscellaneous folder or individual folder for the name of the company.

3. When a letter is of a personal nature, it is coded by using the name of the individual correspondent even though the name of a company appears on the communication as a part of the letterhead, the heading, or the signature of an incoming letter, or as a part of the inside address of an outgoing letter.

4. If a special folder for a special subject is provided in the file, all correspondence pertaining to that subject, regardless of the names of those writing the letters, must be coded with the caption of the special folder in which it will be filed. For example, letters to and from an applicant for a position, and letters to and from third persons or companies in regard to the applicant are coded "Applications."

Methods of Coding Three common methods of coding letters for an alphabetic filing system are described below:

1. The file clerk draws a line with a colored pencil under the entire name of the person, business, or organization that is to serve as a basis for filing, or she may simply underscore the first filing unit of such a name.

2. If the name under which the letter is to be filed does not appear on the letter, that name should be written at the top or in the upper right-hand corner of the communication. For example, a business letter which is written on plain stationery that does not indicate the name of the business and which is signed by an individual would be coded by writing the name of the business at the top of the letter.

3. If a letter is to be filed under a special subject title that does not appear on the letter, the subject title should be written at the top or in the upper right-hand corner of the communication. In addition, the name under which the communication should be filed in the subject folder should be underscored. For example, a letter pertaining to an application for employment (whether it is an actual letter of application or a letter of recommendation) would be coded (1) by writing the word "Applications" at the top of the letter to indicate the title of the folder in which the letter should be filed and (2) by underscoring the applicant's name to show the name to be considered when the letter is placed in the Applications folder.

Cross Referencing When the file clerk codes a letter, she also decides whether or not a cross reference is necessary. If there is a possibility that a letter may be called for by a name other than the one under which it may be filed, the file clerk (1) writes that name in the margin of the letter, or if the name appears in the letter underscores it and writes an "x" in the margin, and (2) prepares a *cross-reference sheet.*

An example of the use of a cross-reference sheet is found in the case of branch office correspondence. If a letter that is received from the branch office of a company contains, in part, information about a customer, the name of the customer is underscored and an "x" is written in either side margin opposite the name to indicate that it will be used for a cross reference. Then the original letter is filed in the Branch Office folder, a cross-reference sheet is made out in the name of the customer, and the cross-reference sheet is filed with the customer's correspondence. This method of handling such a communication allows the filing of the branch office correspondence in one place, and also makes complete the correspondence with and about the customer. Anyone who looks in the folder of correspondence with the customer will find the cross-reference sheet and will know that additional information concerning the customer can be found in the Branch Office folder.

A cross-reference sheet is used when a cross reference to one piece of correspondence is necessary. If a permanent cross reference to a number of pieces of correspondence in the files is desired, it is better to use a visible *cross-reference card.* This is a manila card of the same size as a guide, with a tab in the same position as that used for the tabs of individual folders. The notation on such a tab might be as follows:

Adams & Smith
See Suburban Manufacturing Co.

An example of a situation in which this type of cross reference is used is as follows: The name of the correspondent is changed from Adams & Smith to the Suburban Manufacturing Co. Therefore a new folder is opened for the new name of the company, and all the correspondence is

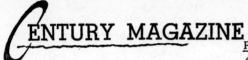

CENTURY MAGAZINE

PEERLESS PUBLISHING COMPANY

X

42 West Muskegon Avenue

DETROIT 3, MICHIGAN

August 12, 19—

mL

AUG 15 2 43 PM 19—

National Office Supply Company
214 New Britain Avenue
San Francisco 5, California

Gentlemen:

When you have established your office in Detroit,
you will be interested in an advertising service
that we offer.

We know business conditions in and around Detroit,
and we can give you a reliable estimate of the
need for your particular type of business in this
region. Our files contain tabulations of business
surveys, made over a period of years, which include
data gathered in the spring of this year.

Century advertising is read by 20,000 business and
professional men in the Detroit area. This market
is open to you through Century, and the services
of our research department are always at your dis-
posal. You will find these an invaluable aid to
starting your business in the Great Lakes area.

A list of our advertising rates is enclosed, along
with a reply envelope for your use.

We hope that we can serve you soon.

Sincerely yours,

D. J. Barron

D. J. Barron, President

cJ

Enclosures 2

Illustration 6B, Letter Coded for Filing and Cross Referencing

CROSS-REFERENCE SHEET

Name or Subject _Peerless Publishing Co._
Detroit, Michigan

Date of Item _August 12, 19--_

Regarding _Advertising rates and research services of Century Magazine_

SEE

Name or Subject _Century Magazine_

Authorized by _Claire Maddox_ Date _Aug. 16, 19--_

Illustration 6C, Cross-Reference Sheet for an Alphabetic File

transferred from the old folder to the new one. The old folder is removed from the file, and in its place is inserted a visible cross-reference card with a tab marked in the manner shown near the bottom of page 55.

Experience alone will indicate to the file clerk the extent to which cross-reference sheets need to be prepared. It is a waste of time to prepare numerous cross-reference sheets or cards if they are not used. It is, however, better to cross-reference too much than too little.

Sometimes one or more extra carbon copies of a letter are made so that each copy may be filed separately. This eliminates the necessity of cross referencing in some cases.

Sorting *Sorting* is the preliminary arrangement of materials in preparation for filing. It serves two purposes. First, it saves time in filing. If the materials were not sorted, it would be necessary for the file clerk to move unsystematically from one file drawer to another. Second, sorting facilitates the location of material that is requested before it has been filed.

Correspondence and cross-reference sheets may be sorted by means of such special equipment as sorting trays or compartments. Equipment of this kind provides spaces, labeled alphabetically or otherwise to fit the filing system in use, into which the materials may be put for preliminary alphabetic arrangement and temporary housing until they are filed.

If special sorting equipment is not available, the materials may be sorted on a desk or table by the file clerk. The steps in this type of sorting are:

1. Sorting the materials into a small number of piles according to the first letters of the first filing units, for example, into five piles: A-C, D-H, I-M, N-S, T-Z.
2. Sorting the materials in each of these five piles into single alphabetic units (A, B, C for the first group) according to the first letters in the first filing units. In performing this step with the T-Z pile, the clerk may put in one pile all correspondence beginning with "X," "Y," or "Z."
3. Sorting the materials in each pile in alphabetic order. Steps 1 and 2 constitute what is known as *rough sorting*. Step 3 is known as *fine sorting*.

—Globe-Wernicke

Illustration 6D, Correspondence Sorter

Before the sorted materials are filed, they may be combined into one or more alphabetically arranged groups.

Placing Corre-   After the correspondence has been
spondence in Folders   sorted alphabetically, it is filed. There
are four steps in this procedure, which are followed for each piece to be filed.

1. The file clerk locates the appropriate drawer by examining the drawer labels. These labels indicate the alphabetic range of materials housed in a particular file drawer.
2. The file clerk scans the guides in the drawer to determine which guide indicates the alphabetic section in which a particular letter should be filed.
3. The file clerk then looks to see whether there is an individual or special folder for the letter. If there is such a folder, the letter is filed in it.
4. If there is no individual or special folder for the letter, the clerk files the letter in the miscellaneous folder in the section. This is usually the last folder in the section.

All correspondence is placed in folders with the letterhead at the left side and the writing facing forward. A paper that is too large for the folder should be folded. Half sheets can be laid side by side so that the folder will not bulge at one end.

In an individual folder the correspondence is arranged according to the date written, with the latest date forward.

In a special folder, such as an Applications folder, the correspondence is placed in strict alphabetic order according to the names of the individuals or companies concerned, and then according to date in each group, with the latest date forward.

In a miscellaneous folder the correspondence is placed in strict alphabetic order according to the names of the individuals or companies concerned, and then according to the date in each group, with the latest date forward. In a miscellaneous folder marked "Br," letters from the following firms would be filed in this manner (reading from the front of the folder to the back):

Correspondents' Names	Dates on Letters
Bradford Company (The)	May 26, 19--
Bradford Company (The)	May 20, 19--
Branch, Charles	July 20, 19--
Brubacker Electric Company	July 30, 19--
Brubacker Electric Company	July 26, 19--
Brubacker Electric Company	April 1, 19--

The Bradford Company letter of May 26 is first in the folder because (1) "Bradford" comes first in the alphabetic order, before "Branch" or "Brubacker," and (2) of the letters received from the Bradford Company, the one dated the 26th is the later.

If the files consist of a number of drawers in a number of cabinets, and if the number of letters filed at one time is quite large, this step of placing correspondence in folders is facilitated by the use of a *file shelf*. By placing the material to be filed on the shelf, which fastens to the side of the open drawer or on the front handle of an adjacent closed drawer, the operator's hands are free to lift folders out of the drawer and place papers properly in the folders.

Adding Individual or Special Folders When correspondence is first carried on with an individual or firm, it is usually placed in a miscellaneous folder along with correspondence pertaining to other companies. As the correspondence with an individual or a firm becomes active

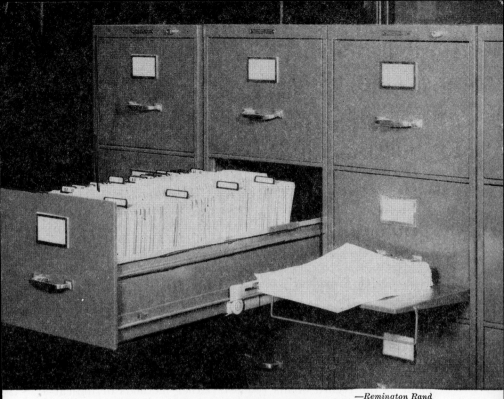

Illustration 6E, File Shelf

and increases in volume, it becomes increasingly difficult to find a particular letter. Since it is not feasible to keep such a volume of material in a miscellaneous folder, individual folders are opened for the active correspondents and all file materials for active correspondents are then transferred from the miscellaneous folder to the new individual folders.

Each office has its own rules regarding the minimum number of pieces of correspondence that justify the opening of an individual folder. Quite frequently the minimum number is six. An individual folder for a correspondent may be opened when the number of pieces of accumulated correspondence is less than the minimum if it is known that the correspondence with that individual or company will be active or is considered important enough to be referred to frequently. There is no rigid rule for this procedure, however. When it is known that correspondence will not continue to be active or when it is not classified as important, an individual folder may not be opened even when the minimum number of pieces of correspondence has been accumulated.

Removing Folders from the File Ordinarily when a request is made for material that has been filed, the folder containing that material is removed from the file; in its place is put a marker known as an *out guide*.

Illustration 6F, Requisition Card

This is a pressboard guide that has a tab that is visible when the guide is placed in the file drawer. On the tab is printed the word "Out." One type of out guide has a printed form on which are written the name of the person borrowing the folder, the date on which the folder was borrowed, and other information pertaining to the folder that has been borrowed. A second type of out guide has a pocket near the top into which is placed a slip or card, known as a *requisition card*. The requisition card is filled out by the person requesting the folder and is sent to the filing department as the record of his request. Other methods of indicating materials that have been removed from the file drawer will be discussed in Chapter 8.

Illustration 6G, Out Guide

QUESTIONS

1. What is a time stamp?
2. What is the purpose of a release mark? Of what may a release mark consist?
3. Is a release mark placed on every piece of correspondence to be filed?
4. To what does the term "inspection" refer?
5. What is meant by the term "coding"?
6. When is the name of the business usually coded?
7. If an incoming business letter does not show the name of the business, under what name is the letter coded (a) if the name of the company is known? (b) if the name of the company is not known?
8. Under what name is a letter of a personal nature coded when it contains the name of the company of the writer?
9. Do special folders contain letters from more than one individual or firm? Give an example.
10. How does a file clerk code a letter that is to be filed under the name given in the letterhead on which it is written?
11. Explain how a letter of application is coded.
12. Explain how a letter of recommendation is coded.
13. What is a cross-reference sheet? Give an example of its use.
14. What is a visible cross-reference card? Give an example of its use.
15. Why is the sorting step desirable?
16. Are cross-reference sheets sorted by themselves or with the correspondence?
17. How does the file clerk locate the folder in which a piece of correspondence should be filed?
18. How is correspondence placed in an individual folder? in a special folder? in a miscellaneous folder?
19. When are individual folders ordinarily opened?
20. What is an out guide?
21. What is a requisition card?

JOB 4—ALPHABETIC CORRESPONDENCE FILING

At this time complete Job 4 in FILING OFFICE PRAC-TICE, Second Edition. The instructions and supplies for this job are included in the practice set.

Chapter 7

TYPES OF ALPHABETIC FILING SYSTEMS

Common Arrangements of Guides and Folders In an alphabetic system of filing the arrangement of guides and folders may take any one of several forms. The form decided upon depends primarily upon the type of business, the volume of correspondence, and any problems that are peculiar to a particular organization.

Three commonly used arrangements of guides and folders in alphabetic filing systems, in addition to the one explained in Chapter 5, are:

1. Primary guides are staggered in first and second positions; the miscellaneous folders, which have the same notations as the primary guides, are staggered in these same two positions; special guides are placed in third position; and individual folders, with tabs that are double width, are placed in last position.

2. Primary guides are in first position; miscellaneous folders are in second position; individual folders occupy third and fourth positions; and special guides and folders are in fifth position.

3. Miscellaneous folders are in first position; primary guides are staggered in second and third positions; individual folders are cut to fourth and fifth positions; special guides and folders are in a sixth position that results from a slight overlapping of tabs throughout the first five positions.

Single and Closed Notations on Guide and Folder Tabs A *single notation,* such as A, Am, B, Be, C, indicates the beginning letter or letters of an alphabetic section in a file. (See Illustration 5J, p. 47.) Several of the commercial systems use tabs marked with closed notations. *Closed* or *double notations* indicate the beginning and ending letters of an alphabetic file section. These may be in the form of E-F, I-J, K-L; or A-Ak, An-Ar, Bo-Bz. Such notations have the advantage of showing the entire alphabetic range covered by the guide or folder bearing them. When such notations are used, the file clerk need not look at the tab on the next guide or folder in order to determine the last letter covered by a preceding guide or folder. However, they also have the disadvantages of being more difficult to read at a glance than are single notations and of making it more difficult to expand the file by adding new guides and miscellaneous folders.

A special type of closed notation, called a *multiple closed notation*, is made up of the letters showing the beginning and the end of an alphabetic section and, in addition, the most frequently used part of this section. For example, the multiple closed notation A-Ad-Ae indicates that the section begins with A and ends with Ae, and that a frequently used part is the Ad division. Multiple closed notations on tabs may also be made as shown at the right. This particular  notation means that the section goes from Aa to Ald and that it includes the important divisions Ak and Ala.

Individual Filing Systems   A filing system for individual office needs can be planned and constructed if certain kinds of equipment are used. Both guides and folders are now made with transparent tabs so that printed or typed slips can be inserted into them. It is also possible to purchase and use gummed labels for the folders of an individual system. By using this type of equipment, it is possible for a trained person to arrange guides and folders in a desired manner and to type notations on insert slips and put these slips into guide and folder tabs.

Commercial Filing Systems   The manufacturers of the various filing systems use arrangements of guides and folders that they consider best from the standpoint of speed in filing and finding material in the files. In brief, it may be said that commercial systems have improved alphabetic filing methods by (1) combining alphabetic notations and numeric symbols to make a double check against misfiling, (2) arranging guides and folders within the file drawer so that maximum visibility is provided, (3) making provisions for special sections of various kinds, and (4) adding color schemes to guide and folder tabs.

The manufactured, or "ready made," alphabetic systems that are discussed in the remaining pages of this chapter are the Standard Alphabetic Expanding System, the Safeguard Filing Plan, the Variadex, the Super-Ideal Index, the

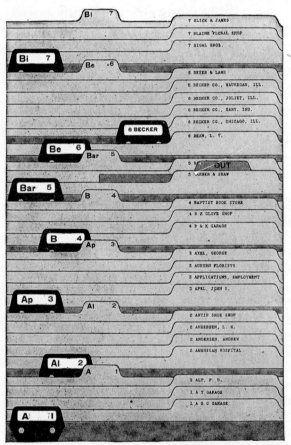

—*Automatic File & Index Co*

Illustration 7A, Standard Alphabetic
Expanding System

Tailor-Made Index, the Yawman and Erbe Direct-Name Index, and the Triple Check Automatic Index.

Standard Alphabetic   This system is made by the Automatic
Expanding System   File & Index Company, of Chicago,
                          Illinois, and Green Bay, Wisconsin.
The system is simple but effective in the arrangement of guides and folders and in the use of simplified notations.

The tabs of the guides and folders are cut to make the equivalent of six positions across the file drawer. Primary guides are staggered in first and second positions; miscellaneous folders are in third position; special and section guides are in fourth position (in the illustration notice the special guide labeled "Becker"); and individual folders are in last position. The tabs of the individual folders are cut to double width so that they actually occupy fifth and sixth positions. (Note the out card in last position.)

Another feature of this system is the use of section numbers, which are included with the alphabetic notations on the guide and folder tabs. This plan makes more rapid filing possible and also serves as a check against the misfiling of folders.

Safeguard   The Safeguard Alphabetic Plan is made by the
Alphabetic   Globe-Wernicke Company, of Cincinnati, Ohio.
Plan   This system, illustrated on page 68, presents a
                 well-planned color scheme for guide and folder
tabs, as well as a scientific arrangement of guides and folders throughout the file drawer.

Primary guides (colored green) and miscellaneous folders (colored red) are staggered in the first three positions. Fourth position is used for special name or title guides, date section guides, and alphabetic breakdown section guides. These sections are blocked out in different colors—yellow for one, orange for another, and so on. In Illustration 7B, page 68, notice the special sections for "Cooper" and for "Flynn." Individual folders with double-width tabs appear in last position and are grouped into color blocks as an aid to filing and finding.

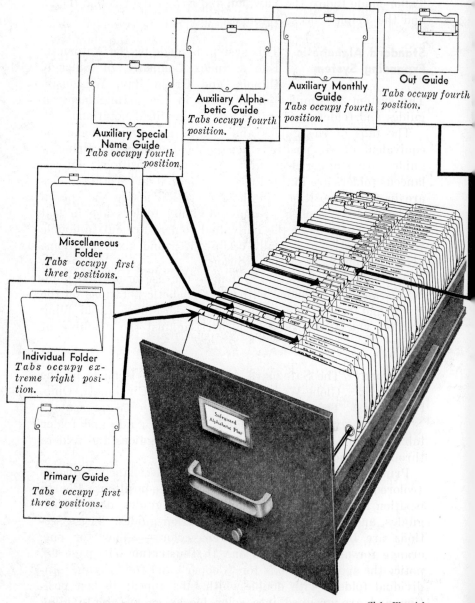

Auxiliary Special Name Guide
Tabs occupy fourth position.

Auxiliary Alphabetic Guide
Tabs occupy fourth position.

Auxiliary Monthly Guide
Tabs occupy fourth position.

Out Guide
Tabs occupy fourth position.

Miscellaneous Folder
Tabs occupy first three positions.

Individual Folder
Tabs occupy extreme right position.

Primary Guide
Tabs occupy first three positions.

—*Globe-Wernicke*

Illustration 7B, Safeguard Alphabetic Plan

The guide tabs are made of celluloid and are arranged so that labels with the desired notations can be inserted into them. Individual folders are marked by typing the company names on gummed labels; each label is then glued over the folder tab.

The primary guides and miscellaneous folders have single notations.

Each alphabetic section is numbered—A 1, B 2, C 3,—to give an additional check against misfiling.

Variadex System   The Variadex System is made by Reming-
ton Rand, Inc., of Buffalo, New York. It is an alphabetic arrangement of guides and folders with a definite color scheme that serves as an auxiliary aid to filing and finding. (See Illustration 7C, page 70.)

In this system first position is reserved for primary guides, which are marked with single notation captions. Second position is used for miscellaneous folders, which show notations similar to those on the guides they follow. Individual folders with two-cut width tabs are placed in third position. Fourth position is used for special guides that mark the location of very active individual folders in third position. OUT guides are also placed in fourth position.

Color is used on the tabs of the guides and on the tab labels for folders and is based upon the second letters of the first indexing units of names to be filed. The colors are determined according to the chart given below.

If the second letter is:	The color on the guide and folder tabs for that section will be:
a, b, c, or d	orange
e, f, g, or h	yellow
i, j, k, l, m, or n	green
o, p, or q	blue
r, s, t, u, v, w, x, y, or z	violet

NOTE: If the first unit of a name does not contain a second letter, as in XYZ Corporation, orange is used. Also, orange is used when single letters appear on guide tabs.

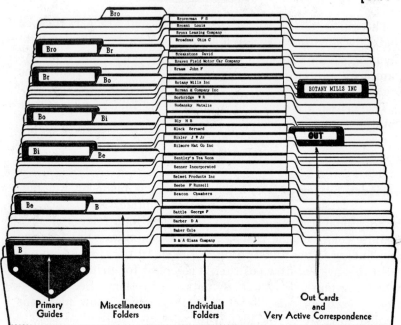

—*Remington Rand*

Illustration 7C, Variadex System

If a guide bears a caption such as Je, the tab will be yellow; if it bears a caption such as Ko, the tab will be blue. If a guide bears a caption consisting of a single letter, the tab is orange.

The tab label of an individual folder is colored according to the second letter in the caption. For example, all folders with captions containing "a" as the second letter are orange; all folders with captions containing "e" as the second letter are yellow; all folders with captions containing "n" as the second letter are green.

Miscellaneous folders in second position are colored to match the guides to which they correspond.

The principle of color is applied when an individual folder is opened for a correspondent. The principle of color is not strictly applied in the miscellaneous folders, however, because these folders bear the same color as the guides they follow even though they may contain correspondence with second letters that would call for different colors on individual folder labels. For example, if sufficient correspondence with John Loso has accumulated in the *orange* miscellaneous L folder, an individual *blue* folder should be opened for him because the second letter in his name is "o."

Yawman and Erbe Direct-Name Index   In this system, numbered folders in first and last positions are filed behind numbered alphabetic guides in second and third positions. The tabs of guides with odd numbers are in the second position, and those with even numbers are in third position.

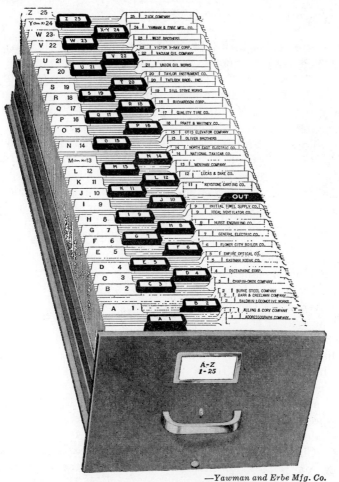

—*Yawman and Erbe Mfg. Co.*

Illustration 7D, Direct-Name Index

In first position are tabs of miscellaneous folders or alphabetic folders printed in red with the same numbering and alphabetic headings as the guides which precede them. Active correspondents are assigned individual folders with double width tabs at the right of the drawer. Each tab shows the name of the correspondent and the number of the guide behind which the folder is filed. When correspondence with a company becomes so voluminous that it must be placed in several folders, a guide marked with the name of the company is placed in front of these folders.

Shaw-Walker Super-Ideal These systems are made by the
and Tailor-Made Indexes Shaw-Walker Company, of Muskegon, Michigan. Super-Ideal is a simple and well-arranged system for alphabetic filing. Primary guides, with multiple closed notations, are staggered in first and second positions (see No. 1 in Illustration 7E). Miscellaneous alphabetic folders, with multiple closed notations, are in first position (No. 2 in the illustration). Individual folders occupy the third and fourth positions (No. 3 in the illustration). Special name guides (No. 4) with wide metal tabs are provided in the fourth position for indexing active accounts, which are filed in individual folders with wide tabs occupying the second, third, and fourth positions (No. 5). Gummed labels (No. 6) with identifying color stripes are available for labeling the individual folders. An out guide (No. 7) is substituted for an individual folder that has been removed from the file drawer.

One drawer set of the Super-Ideal Index consists of approximately 25 primary guides, 20 alphabetic folders, 5 name guides, and 50 individual folders.

The Super-Ideal Index is designed for regular filing and consequently does not provide for such special sections as those that are available with the Shaw-Walker Tailor-Made Index.

The Tailor-Made Index is a much more detailed system and provides for title sections, date sections, follow-up sections (see Chapter 8), and even geographic sections. The notations on guide and miscellaneous folder tabs are multiple closed.

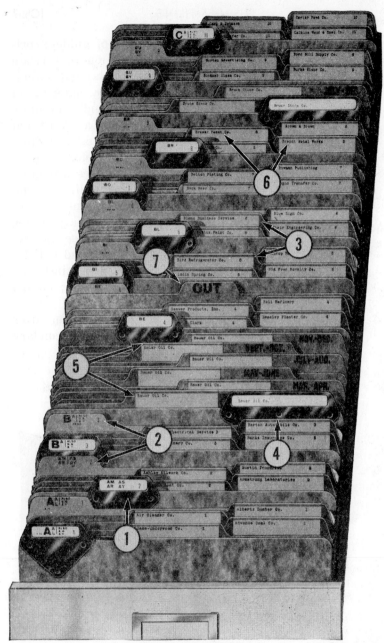

Illustration 7E, Super-Ideal Index

Triple Check
Automatic Index

This system has two sets of guides: primary guides in first position that relate to the first filing units in titles and secondary guides in second position that subdivide the materials in back of the primary guides according to the second filing units in titles. The tabs of the primary guides, such as A 10 and B 20, are numbered according to a chart for coding first filing units, and come in varying divisions of the alphabet to fit individual files. The tabs of the secondary guides are numbered consecutively according to a chart for coding second filing units. A uniform set of secondary guides, nine in number and ranging from A to Z, follows each primary guide. In a set of nine secondary guides, there are three groups. Each group of three guides, such as A-B 11, C 12, and D-F 13, is a different color to provide an additional check against misfiling. The labels on the first three guides are tan; on the second three, green; and on the last three, yellow.

A miscellaneous folder is placed in third position after each guide. The miscellaneous folders behind secondary

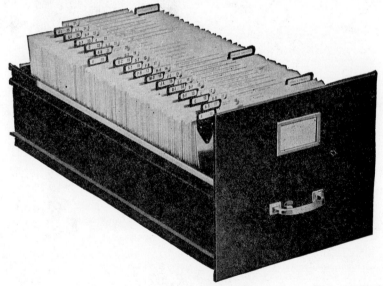

—Remington Rand

Illustration 7F, Triple Check Automatic Index

guides bear the same tab notations as the secondary guides they follow; the miscellaneous folders behind primary guides bear the same *numeric* tab notations as the primary guides they follow and, instead of the same alphabetic notations, the words "Single Name or Subject." These are special folders for materials concerning subjects or single-name correspondents. Such materials are filed in alphabetic order in these folders.

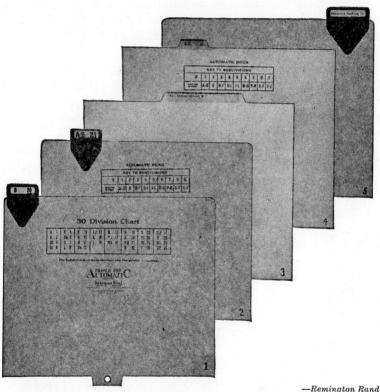

—*Remington Rand*

Illustration 7G, Guides and Folders in Triple Check Automatic Index

Individual folders are placed in fourth position in front of miscellaneous folders. Individual folders that follow secondary guides are the same color as those secondary guides; individual folders that follow primary guides are not colored since these guides are white. Since individuals folders following one guide have the same code number, they must be arranged alphabetically within their own group.

The last position, at the right of the file drawer, is reserved for special name guides and out guides.

Illustration 7G, on page 75, shows the types of guides and folders, except the "Single Name or Subject" folder, used in this system. The tab of the "Single Name or Subject" folder is cut for third position and is placed immediately behind the first-position primary guide.

The Triple Check Automatic Index is essentially a double alphabetic arrangement with alphabetic divisions of first and second filing units. The numbering system is used to speed up filing since filing by number is more rapid than filing by letters of the alphabet. Once the file operator has become familiar with this numbering system, she can code and file the material rapidly.

The chart on which the numbering system for the primary guides is based is as follows (the guides are numbered in groups of 10's, from A 10 to XYZ 300) :

30-Division Chart for Primary Code Numbers

A	10	H	110	P-Q	210
		Ho	120		
B	20			R	220
Bi	30	I-J	130		
Br	40			S	230
		K	140	Si	240
C	50			St	250
Co	60	L	150		
D	70			T	260
		M	160		
		Me	170	U-V	270
E	80	Mo	180		
				W	280
F	90	N	190	Wi	290
G	100	O	200	XYZ	300

The chart on which the numbering system for the secondary guides is based is as follows:

Chart for Secondary Code Numbers

A-B	1	G-I	4	P-R	7
C	2	J-L	5	S-T	8
D-F	3	M-O	6	U-Z	9

Single Name or Subject   0

In checking the following examples of coding, follow the procedure by comparing the examples with the primary and secondary charts given above.

Example 1. Correspondence from John Allen is coded 15 (10 for *Allen* plus 5 for *John*) and is filed in an individual folder numbered 15 behind the J-L 15 guide or in the miscellaneous folder marked J-L 15 in the A-10 section.

Example 2. Correspondence pertaining to applications is coded 10 (10 for *Applications*) and is filed in an individual folder numbered 10 behind the A-10 guide or in the Single Name or Subject 10 folder in the A-10 section.

Example 3. Correspondence from a firm named Childs is coded 50 and is filed in an individual folder numbered 50 behind the C-50 guide or in the Single Name or Subject folder in the front of the C-50 section. Since there is no second filing unit in this name, the primary guide is the only guide used in determining the filing position.

Example 4. Correspondence from the Charles F. Collins Company is coded 62 (60 for *Collins* plus 2 for *Charles*) and is filed in an individual folder numbered 62 behind the C-62 guide or in the miscellaneous folder marked C 62 in the Co-60 section.

Exception. The one type of name that presents a variation from these rules is a title beginning with a compound geographic name. For example, in Triple Check Automatic Coding "New York" is considered as one filing unit and is given the code for "N"; the next word in the title is considered as the second filing unit and is given a code number from the chart for secondary code numbers. In the alphabetic arrangement of folders behind any one guide, each word in a compound geographic name is considered a separate indexing unit. This rule for coding compound geographic names does not affect alphabetic arrangement of folders or papers in folders.

The following names indicate this principle of coding and filing geographic names. The four names "North Carolina Insurance Co.," "North Central Gas & Electric Co.," "North Chicago Home Builders, Inc.," and "Gary Northrup" have the same code—194. The folders bearing these names are arranged according to the regular rules for alphabetic filing. "North Carolina Insurance Co." is first; "North Central Gas & Electric Co." is second; "North Chicago Home Builders, Inc.," is third; and "Gary Northrup" is fourth.

Departments of the federal government are indexed under "United States Government" as the first unit and the name of the department as the second unit. For example, the code number for the United States Department of Commerce is 272, with "United States Government" the first unit and "Commerce" the second.

The chart for primary code numbers, given at the bottom of page 76, is based on thirty primary guides to the filing system (hence thirty divisions in the system). As the size of the system increases, and as more guides are used (forty, sixty, or more), a different primary code number chart must be used.

QUESTIONS

1. Upon what factors does the arrangement of guides and folders in an alphabetic filing system depend?
2. What are single notations? Give an example.
3. What are closed notations? Give an example.
4. What are multiple closed notations? Give an example.
5. What items of equipment are used in constructing an individual filing system?
6. How have commercial systems improved alphabetic filing methods?
7. For what purposes are the various positions used in the Standard Alphabetic Expanding System?
8. How is color used in the Safeguard Filing Plan?
9. For what purposes are the various positions in the Variadex System used?
10. How is color used in the Variadex System to facilitate filing?

11. Describe the Super-Ideal Index.
12. Give some of the ways in which the Tailor-Made Index differs from the Super-Ideal Index.
13. What are the purposes of each set of guides in the Triple Check Automatic Index?
14. What kinds of folders are used in the Triple Check Automatic Index?
15. For what are the two charts in the Triple Check Automatic Index used?

PROBLEMS

1. Using the charts for Triple Check Automatic Index presented on pages 76 and 77, code the following names and arrange them in the order they would appear in a file.

A B C Moving & Storage, Inc.
John Benny's Trucking Service
Charles Walker, Sr., Trucking Service
Carter-De Camp Express Company
Elk Transportation Co., Inc.

Master Trucking Company
Cole Trucking Company
J T Auto Trucking
Mid-States Freight Lines, Inc.
Gross Transportation Corp.

Gray Fleet Trucking Co.
12 Main Street, Albany

McMillian Express Co.
A A Truck Renting Corp.

Mar-Lin Trucking Co.
D'Angelo Bros., Inc.
Inter State Movers
F C J Trucking Co.
Davis-Morton's Stores, Inc.

Tri-Us Motor Delivery, Inc.
Elmhurst Van & Storage Co.
J & M O'Neil, Inc.
Mark Carriers Co.
W. J. Casey Trucking Co., Inc.

Raymond Davis Parcel System
Ace Express Company Rochester, New York
Sol's Trucking Corp.

K & S Trucking Co.

Gray Fleet Trucking Co.
14 Main Avenue, New Haven

Benny's Fast Freight
Tri-Boro Transportation Corp.
M. M. Richards, Inc.
Ace Express Company Cloverdale, Indiana

Southern Motor Express Co.
Gross Freight Line, Inc.
Spencer & Robbins Express
Home Storage & Warehouse Co.
Aceste Trucking Co.

Interstate Motor Freight System
McManus Delivery Agency
Trio Motor Lines
Walter Carter Moving & Expressing
Midwest Freight Forwarding Co.

The Long Transportation Company
Frank McManus
J. R. Coleman Express Co.
McIntosh Freight Lines, Incorporated
F & F Trucking Co.

Marvin M. Richards Transportation Service
Jack's Trucking Co.
New York Rigging Service

2. Arrange the following list of names in alphabetic order and then indicate the color that would be used on the guides and folder tabs if the Variadex System were being used.

Bob-Jules Musical Instruments
Jimmy's Music Shop, Inc.
Ye Olde Music Shoppe
Musical Instrument Exchange
Lyon & Healy Harp Salon

Fischer Radios
   22 Ocean Street
   Baton Rouge, La.
Link-Jayman Mouthpieces
Louis Kramer Violins, Inc.

J. T. Serry School of
   Accordion
Manny's Musical Accessories
Carroll Musical Instrument
   Service
B. Newman & Sons
W. L. Tompkins, III, Music
   Supplies

M. Hayes Accordion Head-
   quarters
West & Williams Drum Shop
Walter de La Roche Music
   Center
Unredeemed Pledge Sales Co.,
   Inc.
Easton-Rogers Music Inc.

Arthur del Rose Music Corp.
Charles R. Point Music Co.
Heights Music Service, Inc.
Terminal Music Corp.
Wel-Come Music Store

Martin Guitars
Link & Long Band Instruments
Fred de La Hart Instrument
   Co.
N Y Band Instrument Co., Inc.

Ross-Hayes Music Shop
Silver & Harper Pianos
Universal Musical Instrument
   Co.

Fischer Bros. Music Exchange
International Percussion
   Supplies
Richard Tompkins, Inc.
York Bank Instrument Co.,
   Inc.
Excelsior Guitars, Inc.

Fischer Radios
   49 Clay Street
   Richmond, Virginia
Opperman Brothers Woodwinds,
   Inc.
Eddie Belle Guitar Head-
   quarters

J & S Ross Band Instruments
Symphonia Musical Supply
   Company
Favorite Music Mfg. Co.
George Carroll Piano Service
O'Sullivan Musical
   Instruments

Bell-Higgins Music Center
G F A Guitar Corp.
Robert H. Young Music
   Supplies
Treasure Thrift Music
   Accessories
Karl A. Berger, Jr., Music
   Co.

Avery Henry Music Co.
A C E Accordion Co.

Chapter 8

CHARGE AND FOLLOW-UP METHODS

Need for Charge and Follow-Up Placing materials in the files by any one of the methods described in the preceding chapters is only a means to an end. The purpose of systematic filing is to make materials readily available for use when they are needed. To accomplish this purpose, it is as necessary to be systematic in removing materials from the files as it is in placing them there.

If filing is to remain systematic, controls must be maintained in the following steps:

1. The procedure by which materials are requested from the files.
2. The handling of the request so that the materials will be made available at the time they are needed.
3. The charging of the materials to the individual to whom they are released.
4. The follow-up by the filing department to make sure that borrowed materials are returned in a reasonable time.

Requisition Methods

Use of Requisition Cards A special form for each item or folder of material that is requested is used in this method. The form, known as a *requisition card,* provides space for identifying the materials requested and the individual or department making the request, and for noting the date on which the request was made and the date on which the material is delivered. A five- by three-inch requisition card is shown in Illustration 6F on page 62.

In some offices the requisition card is made out by the individual or department making the request for materials from the files. In other offices the request is communicated to the filing department, either in person or by telephone, and the requisition card is completed in the filing department.

81

Use of   If it is known at the time materials are
Tickler Files   being released for filing that they will be
                    needed again at some future date, such
materials can be appropriately marked or stamped before
being routed to the filing department. One of the following
notations may be used for this coding: "Pending," "Follow-
Up," "Date Ahead," or "Tickler" with the date when the
material is desired. When the file clerk inspects and codes
these materials for filing or when she receives a request for
future delivery of filed materials, she fills out a requisition
card for each item or folder. These cards are filed in a special
date card file called a *tickler* or *follow-up file*.

The guide system for a tickler or follow-up file may consist
of twelve monthly primary guides and a set of thirty-one daily
secondary guides. The latter are used to subdivide the primary monthly sections of the file. Usually only one set of
daily guides is needed because these can be moved forward
and used over again from month to month. The requisition
cards are filed behind the appropriate monthly and daily
guides according to the dates on which the materials in the
files are requested. Each day the file clerk removes the requisition cards from behind the guide for the current date to
determine which papers or folders are needed for the day.

Charge Methods

Out Guide When the requisition card calls for the entire con-
               tents of a folder, three methods of charging the
material to the borrower are commonly used. One method
makes use of an *out guide*. This is a pressboard guide with
an "Out" caption on a fifth-cut tab and with a pocket on the
front side to hold the requisition card. An out guide is shown
in Illustration 6G, page 62. The file clerk inserts the requisition card in the pocket of the out guide and puts the guide in
the space formerly occupied by the borrowed folder. Thus,
the "out" guide serves as a marker for the missing folder, and
the requisition card in the "out" guide pocket serves to identify
and charge the borrower.

Illustration 8A, Card Tickler with One Form of Requisition

Out Folder   A second method is that of using an *out folder*. Such a folder is substituted for the folder that is removed from the file and is used to hold filed materials during the time that the borrowed folder is out of the file drawer. In this method a substition card, to which the requisition card is attached, is placed in the out folder. Again, the requisition card becomes a charge against the borrower.

Carrier Folder   A third method uses a special *carrier folder* of a distinctive color and marked, "Return to Files." The requested materials are transferred from the regular folder to the carrier folder before they are delivered to the borrower. The requisition card is used with a substitution card in the same manner indicated for the out-folder method.

The carrier-folder method has several advantages: (1) it retains the regular folder for housing materials that may be released to the filing department before the borrowed papers and carrier folder are returned; (2) it reminds the borrower, by means of its distinctive color, that the materials should be returned; (3) it saves the regular folder from the unusual handling to which it would be subjected if it left the filing department.

Out Card   When the request is for a single paper or for part of the contents of a folder, an *out* or *substitution card* holding a charge slip may be inserted in the folder from which the material has been removed. Another *out card* form in general use does not hold a charge slip but has printed lines on which charge information is written.

—*Remington Rand*

Illustration 8B, Out or Substitution Card

Out-Sheet Method   The procedure in this method is very much like that for the card-requisition method. A request for filed materials is made on an out-sheet form which shows data similar to that included on an out-requisition card. When requested material is removed from the files, this sheet is placed in the folder to substitute and charge for the paper or papers that have been removed. Frequently an out folder is placed in the file and the out sheet is put into this folder. Like the requisition card, the out sheet is used in three ways: (1) as a requisition, (2) as a follow-up form for tickler filing, and (3) as a record of a charge for borrowed materials.

A tickler file for out sheets consists of 12 monthly guides and a set of 31 daily folders. This type of folder is commonly known as a *day folder,* and each is printed with a number on a tab to indicate the day of the month.

The particular charge system that is adopted for use by a filing department should indicate clearly the identity of the materials that have been removed from the files and the names of the persons or departments who are using the borrowed materials.

On-Call Cards   When a request for material from the files cannot be filled because the material has been borrowed by someone else, the file clerk may put an on-call card in the folder designated in the requisition. When the requested material is returned to the folder, the on-call card reminds the file clerk that the material should be sent immediately to the person whose name appears on the card.

ON CALL			
Materials Requested		Requested by	
Date	Identification	Date	Name
5/30/–	J. E. Jones letters	6/4/–	H. J. Johnson
6/1/–	Bancroft Co. letters	6/8/–	Walter Banks
6/5/–	Rockwell Co. telegram	6/15/–	John Adams

Illustration 8C, On-Call Card

Follow-Up Methods

Card Tickler If the filing department is small, it is a simple
File matter for the file clerk to check the due dates
of borrowed materials on the requisition cards
or sheets in the main files. If the department is large, however, this follow-up is simplified by the use of a card tickler
file. Under such a plan, when material is removed from the file
and the requisition card is placed in the pocket of an out guide
or attached to a substitution card, a charge copy of the requisition card is prepared and filed in a tickler file according to
the date that the borrowed material should be returned. This
may be a separate file from the one used for filing pending
requisition cards, or one file may be used for both purposes
by separating the requisition cards from the charge cards
behind each daily guide.

Each day the file clerk checks to determine what borrowed
materials are due and notifies the borrower in each case. If
the materials are still needed by the borrower, the due date
on the requisition card is extended; otherwise, the materials
are returned and the charge is canceled.

When borrowed materials are returned, the charge against
the borrower must be canceled. This is done by removing the
out guide or substitution card from the files and destroying
the requisition card held in the pocket of the guide or card.
The copy of the requisition card, if one has been used in the
tickler file for the follow-up of borrowed materials, is also
removed and destroyed.

The Dated Folder Special follow-up folders, called *dated*
Follow-Up Method *folders,* are sometimes used in charge and
follow-up systems. These folders have
a straight-edge back printed from left to right with numbers
from 1 to 31, corresponding to the days of the month. A
movable colored signal is used to indicate the follow-up date
that applies to the folder. When a request is made for the
future delivery of filed material, that material is transferred
immediately from the files to a dated follow-up folder. A
copy of the requisition card or out-sheet is left in the file

in place of the removed material, and a copy is also placed in the follow-up folder along with the requested material. The date of delivery is signaled on the follow-up folder tab, and the folder is placed in the tickler file in its proper position according to the day and month for delivery.

Carbon Follow-Up Method   This method calls for two copies of each outgoing letter, where a follow-up is involved, to be sent to the filing department. The follow-up carbon is often of a different color from the file copy. The follow-up date is marked on the carbon, and this copy is filed according to due date in a file equipped with month and day guides.

Other Uses of Follow-Up Files

The filing department is not the only part of a business that needs and uses follow-up files. In the regular course of business activity in all departments, hundreds of matters arise which involve some future consideration. Attending to these matters at the proper time is a very important responsibility in business and cannot be left safely to the memory of any one person or group of persons. One act of omission may mean the loss of an important customer or the lack of necessary equipment or supplies at a critical time.

Card follow-up systems are widely used in a variety of ways. Dated follow-up cards are used to call to mind appointments, meetings, and telephone calls. Collection departments use follow-up files to indicate dates for checking accounts receivable items that are due. Advertising departments need a follow-up system to mark dates for running certain kinds of advertising copy and for utilizing contracted space in various magazines or newspapers. Sales departments use such files for periodic checks on the progress of sales campaigns and to route sales calls by their representatives.

The use of follow-up files makes for better organization in a business or in a department of a business. A follow-up system makes for orderly procedure and prevents costly errors which occur when important matters for future attention are left to memory.

QUESTIONS

1. How can a letter that is to be released for filing be coded to show that it will be needed at some future time?
2. What is a requisition card?
3. What types of information are recorded on a requisition card?
4. Describe a date file for requisitions.
5. How does a file clerk use a date file for requisitions?
6. In what way is an out guide used?
7. In what way is an out folder used?
8. In what way is a carrier folder used?
9. What is an on-call card?
10. Describe the methods used to insure the return of borrowed material to its file.
11. Describe the carbon follow-up method.
12. In what way is a dated folder used?
13. Give examples of uses made of follow-up files by departments in a business other than the filing department.

JOB 5—REQUISITION AND CHARGE PROCEDURES

At this time complete Job 5 in FILING OFFICE PRAC-TICE, Second Edition. The instructions and supplies for this job are included in the practice set.

Chapter • 9

• TRANSFER METHODS

Need for Transferring Materials

Many materials that are filed are important for reference purposes for a short time only. If materials that have ceased to be important in this respect are permitted to remain in the files indefinitely, the efficiency of the system is reduced. Consequently such materials should be removed from the main files according to some definite plan. They cannot be discarded, however, until they are no longer of any value. It is the function of transfer files to house these materials until they are discarded.

Transferring materials serves the following purposes:

1. It makes for more efficient filing and finding of active materials.
2. It reduces costs by making valuable floor space available for the active files and by allowing the old materials to be housed in less expensive cabinets.
3. It provides storage space for materials that are still valuable although not currently active.

Transfer Equipment and Supplies

Transfer files require less expensive equipment than do the regular files because reference to transferred material is not made nearly so often as to active material. Hence there is no need for ballbearing rollers on cabinet drawers, finely finished outside surfaces, or detailed guides to mark sections in the cabinets. Transfer cases may be constructed of wood or heavy cardboard; at best, they are plainly finished steel units.

Active file guides are not taken with folders when a transfer is made. The guide sets are too expensive and, as a rule, are too detailed for transfer file needs. It is ordinarily advisable to have a single set of guides in transfer cases, although the notations on miscellaneous folders from the regular file may be sufficient for guiding purposes.

Miscellaneous and individual folders are generally transferred from active to transfer files. However, specially made folders (with celluloid tabs or other refinements) are too expensive to be transferred and again replaced in the active files. It is economical to prepare cheaper manila folders for transfer filing purposes.

It is common practice to stamp each folder that is transferred with the words "Transferred File" or some similar notation to prevent transferred folders from being filed in the active file later. Each folder should be marked also with the date of its contents.

Transfer Methods

Several methods of moving papers from the active files to transfer files are used. These methods are classified as (1) perpetual transfer and (2) periodic transfer.

Perpetual Transfer This method consists of constantly removing inactive material from the main files and sending it to the transfer files. It can be used to best advantage when work is completed in units, as in the work of lawyers, contractors, and architects. Individual cases or jobs may be transferred as units as soon as they are completed.

The perpetual transfer is not suited to usual business correspondence because it involves the continual marking of papers for transfer and creates additional work.

Periodic Transfers *Periodic transfer* is the removal of papers at stated intervals. Transfers may be made in one of the following three ways: (1) by the one-period method, (2) by the two-period method, or (3) by the maximum-minimum period method.

One-Period Method. At a certain time (usually once or twice a year) all material is taken from the active files and is sent to the transfer files. A new active file is started at this time. The chief fault of this method is that much active material is transferred, and as a result the transfer files must be consulted too frequently for some time following the transfer.

Two-Period Method. In this method the upper drawers of the file cabinet are used to house current papers, while the lower drawers are kept as a separate file and less active material is filed in them; or filing cabinets are grouped in pairs with one reserved for current materials and the other for semiactive materials. At chosen transfer times the contents of the semiactive files are sent to the transfer files, and materials in the active files are moved to the semiactive files. Thus, if cabinet space permits, semiactive material is available without having to refer to the transfer files. The disadvantage of this method is that it requires three sets of files: the active files for current correspondence, the semiactive files, and the transfer files.

Maximum-Minimum Transfer. A transfer method that eliminates the objectionable features of both the one-period transfer and the two-period transfer is known as the maximum-minimum transfer. When this method is used, only the inactive material is transferred at regular intervals. The following example indicates the operation of the system. In a particular office material is transferred once a year on June 30. All material under the date of the current year is left in the active files and all material under the date of the preceding year is transferred. This means that materials are kept in the active files at least six months (December 31 of the preceding year to June 30 of the year in which the transfer is made) but not more than eighteen months (January 1 of the preceding year to June 30 of the transfer year). In other words, the material that is transferred varies in age at the time of transfer from six to eighteen months. It is from these minimum and maximum periods of time (six months and eighteen months in the example) that this method derives its name.

Other Transfer Problems

Time Limits for Keeping Papers Although some company records have a permanent value, the majority of them have a limited period of usefulness. Every office must act on this matter of the retention of its records. In small offices the executive or his secretary makes this decision.

In large offices it is often done by a records retention committee, composed of an officer of the company, the company's legal counsel, the file supervisor, and, as each department's records come up for review by the committee, the supervisor of that department. This committee is aided in its task by the state statute of limitations, federal laws governing the retention of certain documents, and the current practices in similar lines of business.

Transfer Rooms The space allotted to storage of inactive records should be as close as possible to the active records department in a fireproof building. It should have a person in attendance, if possible. If the room does not have an attendant, it should be kept locked and the filing department staff should assume control of the records. The same rules should apply for maintaining and borrowing transferred material as for active files.

Microphotography as a Transfer Medium Many companies are today microfilming their records, partly to reduce storage space, and partly for protection against possible air attacks. There are many companies offering microfilm equipment and services today, and any business organization undertaking such a program will find the microfilm companies extremely helpful in the development of procedures for using their products.

Illustration 9A, Recordak Reliant Microfilmer

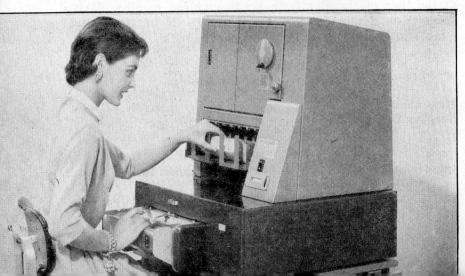

Illustration 9B, Recordak Film Reader

QUESTIONS

1. What purposes are served by the transfer of materials that have been filed?
2. How do transfer files differ from regular files in regard to type and cost?
3. Explain the perpetual transfer method.
4. What is the one-period method of transfer?
5. How many sets of files are needed in the two-period transfer method? Why?
6. Describe the maximum-minimum transfer method.
7. Are transferred records kept indefinitely?
8. Is a charge card made out for material borrowed from the transfer room?
9. Why are records microfilmed?

PROBLEMS

1. The office of the Logan Jewelry Store transfers its correspondence once a year on June 30 according to the two-period method. (a) If a letter is dated July 5, 1955, on what date is it removed to the semiactive files? (b) On what date is it removed to the transfer files?

2. The filing department of the Springfield Service Agency transfers its correspondence twice a year on January 2 and July 1 according to the two-period method. (a) If a letter is dated October 9, 1955, on what date is it removed to the semiactive files? (b) On what date is it removed to the transfer files?

3. The maximum-minimum transfer method is used in the filing department of the Anderson-French Paint Company. On December 31 of each year all correspondence dated on or before June 30 of the current year is transferred to the inactive files. (a) When a letter is transferred, how old is it if it is dated July 1 of the preceding year? (b) April 30 of the current year? (c) December 31 of the preceding year?

4. The office of the Gift Mart transfers its correspondence on July 1 of each year according to the maximum-minimum transfer method. At this time it removes to the transfer files all correspondence of the entire preceding year. (a) What are the minimum and maximum transfer periods under this plan? (b) What is the date of a letter that is transferred on July 1, 1955, if it is ten months old? seven months old? sixteen months old?

5. In the office of the Standard Hardware Company the minimum period is three months, and the maximum period is fifteen months. Upon what date must the transfer be made each year in order that all the material that is transferred will bear one calendar year date?

Chapter • 10

NUMERIC FILING

Nature and Uses of a Numeric File   A numeric file is one in which numbers are used for guide and folder captions. This type of file may be used to advantage under the following circumstances:

1. When file materials concern numbered districts or territories, such as sales districts or distribution areas.
2. When records are kept for numbered items of merchandise and/or reports as well as correspondence concerning such merchandise. Examples are stock records and orders for numbered stock items.
3. When file materials concern contract or job work. For example, a building contractor's files, where each job is a separate unit, should be based on a numeric system so that all materials pertaining to one job may be filed under one primary heading.
4. When file materials concern case histories. For example, cases in a hospital or social service agency, where each case is a unit in itself, are numbered and filed as units.
5. In a law office, where each client is assigned a number and each case handled for the client is assigned a subsidiary number of the main number.

Organization of a Numeric File   A numeric correspondence file usually consists of three parts:

1. A main correspondence file in which guides and folders bear numeric captions.
2. A supplementary card index in which correspondents' names are arranged alphabetically.
3. A miscellaneous alphabetic file in which materials pertaining to inactive correspondence or inactive subjects are housed.

In the main numeric file each important correspondent is given a separate folder that has a numbered caption. The folders are numbered in sequence, beginning with 1 or 101, with little or no regard for the alphabetic order of names. When the volume of letters concerning a correspondent warrants the opening of an individual folder, that folder is given the next unassigned number, which may be determined by consulting the folder and card supply. All materials to, from, or about this correspondent are always placed in this folder, with the most recent material in the front.

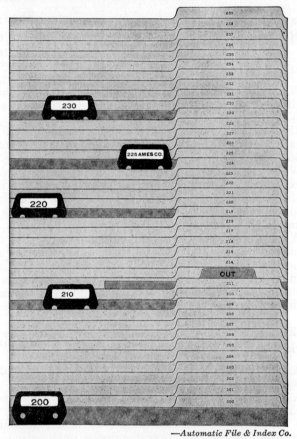

—*Automatic File & Index Co.*

Illustration 10A, Numeric Correspondence File

A number may also be assigned to a subject or group classification such as "Applications." In such a case all materials relating to this subject are filed in the same folder; and within this folder the letters are filed in alphabetic order according to the names of the applicants, and all letters pertaining to one applicant are arranged according to date.

Arrangement of The guides in a numeric file may appear
a Numeric File in any of the available positions. One arrangement of guides and folders in a nu-
meric correspondence file is shown in Illustration 10A. Primary
guides are staggered in the first and second positions; special
guides, for very active correspondents, are placed in third
position; individual folders are placed in last position. The
captions throughout are numeric except in the case of the
special guides, which include the names of the correspondents
as well as the numbers.

In the system shown in the illustration, the guides are numbered by 10's so that only ten folders fall into the numeric
range indicated by each guide. The folders are placed in the
drawer in strict numeric order. The tabs of the folders bear
only the numbers assigned to the various correspondents so
that no correspondents' names are visible except on the special
guides.

Supplementary   Since guide and folder tab notations show
Card Index File only numbers, an alphabetic file card control is essential to the operation of a nu-
meric file. The card control consists of an alphabetic arrangement of the names of the correspondents. The names are
typed on cards which are filed behind alphabetic guides in a
special card drawer or in a file box. Each card gives the
name of a correspondent or a
subject and shows the number
of the folder that has been assigned to that name or subject;
for example, American Paper
Company—folder No. 105.
Thus, if the number of the
folder given to that company
is forgotten, the card will show
that letters to, from, or about
this company are in folder No.
105.

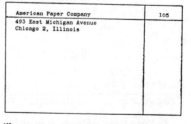

Illustration 10B, Card in the Supplementary Card Index File

The cards in the supplementary card index file are usually
made out like the one in Illustration 10B.

Miscellaneous Alphabetic File Numeric folders are not usually prepared for correspondence that is not active or frequent. Such papers are usually held in a miscellaneous alphabetic file until they accumulate to a point where it is practical to prepare an individual folder for them in the numeric file.

The miscellaneous alphabetic file is usually placed in the front part of the first file drawer of the regular numeric file. However, it may be kept in a separate filing cabinet or drawer. The miscellaneous alphabetic file usually consists of guides and miscellaneous folders with alphabetic captions only.

Materials that are filed in the miscellaneous alphabetic file may or may not be indexed in the supplementary card index file. If a card index is used, each card that serves as an index for this type of material is marked with the letter "M," instead of a number, in the upper right-hand corner to indicate that the correspondence is in the miscellaneous file.

Accession Book or Register Many users of a numeric system keep an accession book or register. This is a consecutive record of numbers assigned, such as the following:

NUMBER	NAME	DATE
1531	Acme Dental Supply Company	10/26/--
1532	Polaroid Company	10/26/--
1533	Comstock, Robert J.	10/27/--
1534		
1535		

Illustration 10C, Accession Register

Numeric Filing Procedure Accuracy in numeric filing requires an understanding of the following steps.

Inspection. Each incoming letter should be checked to see that it has been released for filing.

Preliminary Name Coding. Each letter must be read carefully by the file clerk to determine which name is to be used as a basis for numeric coding. The file clerk must then underscore the name so that she will know that it has been selected as the code name. Other names that will be used for cross-reference purposes should be marked also.

Alphabetic Sorting. After the file clerk has underscored all names to be considered in filing the correspondence, she sorts the pieces of correspondence alphabetically as a preparatory step for the numeric coding process. This step is not necessary if the volume of correspondence is small.

Numeric Coding. The first step in the numeric coding process includes checking in the card file for every name to be coded. If the name appearing on a piece of correspondence is listed in the card file, the file clerk notes the number already assigned to that name and uses it to code the letter. She writes in the upper right-hand corner of the letter the number that has been assigned to that particular correspondent. The file clerk should be absolutely certain to write the correct number in clear, easily read style. Failure to do so may result in the misfiling of correspondence. A careless clerk will sometimes write a digit inaccurately, occasionally drop a digit (record 1597 as 159, for example), and all too often transpose figures (record 467 as 476). Such errors as these make the filing system ineffective.

If no number has been assigned to the correspondent because his correspondence is inactive or new, the letter is coded by writing "M" in the upper right-hand corner to indicate that the letter is to be filed in the miscellaneous alphabetic file. Every piece of correspondence, whether it is an incoming letter or the carbon copy of an outgoing communication, must be coded.

Cross References. Cross references in a numeric system are usually made in the card index file. They are used when a firm is known by two different names or has changed its name, or when individuals connected with the firm are likely to be thought of in connection with the correspondence.

If the American Paper Company, folder No. 105, changes its name to the National Paper Company, a cross-reference card would be made like the one in Illustration 10D, page 100.

National Paper Company	105x
493 East Michigan Avenue Chicago 2, Illinois Successors to American Paper Company	

American Paper Company	105
493 East Michigan Avenue Chicago 2, Illinois National Paper Company, Successors	

Illustration 10D, Cross-Reference Card When All Correspondence Is Filed in Only One Folder

Illustration 10E, Original Card with Notation

The number assigned to the card is 105x to indicate that the number of the folder is 105 and that the card is but a cross-reference card. The additional note, "National Paper Company, Successors," would be typed on the old card of the American Paper Company (Illustration 10E).

If correspondence for the National Paper Company is likely to be called for under the name of Walter Cummings, the president of the company, the cross reference appears as shown in Illustration 10F.

When a piece of correspondence deals with two or more companies or persons for whom there are separate folders, cross-reference cards are also prepared. For example, if some of the correspondence relating to the Globe Insurance Company is filed in the folders for Rand & Sons and for The Scott Insurance Company, the card for the Globe Insurance Company should indicate the numbers of these folders and the names of the companies concerned (Illustration 10G).

Cummings, Walter	105x
 See National Paper Company	

Globe Insurance Company	206
1206 Pennsylvania Avenue Pittsburgh 5, Pennsylvania See Rand & Sons The Scott Insurance Company	321 752

Illustration 10F, Cross-Reference Card for an Individual

Illustration 10G, Cross-Reference Notation When Correspondence Is Filed in More Than One Folder

Numeric Sorting for Filing. After all the communications
have been coded, the file clerk sorts them. She sorts them
first by hundreds, then by tens, and finally by units. All pieces
coded "M" are placed in one pile so that they may be filed at
one time in the miscellaneous alphabetic file.

Placing Material in Folders. All materials bearing code
numbers are placed in folders bearing those same numbers.
If two or more pieces of correspondence have the same code
number, they are placed in the folder according to date, with
the latest date in front.

All materials coded "M" are filed alphabetically in the miscellaneous alphabetic section of the file.

Adding Individual Folders. Individual folders are assigned
only to important correspondents. The reason for this restric-
tion is that it would be too expensive to buy enough folders
so that one could be assigned to every correspondent. Furthermore, a great deal of unnecessary time would be spent in filing
materials if every new piece had to be filed in a separate
folder. The matter of determining which correspondents and
which groups of materials are important enough to warrant
the opening of individual folders is a point each office must
decide for itself.

If a new correspondent is believed to be important, or if
the communications with a correspondent have accumulated
in the miscellaneous alphabetic file to the minimum number
of pieces established by the business for the opening of an
individual folder, the file clerk assigns to that correspondent
the next number that comes after the number of the last
folder in the file. She then codes the communications by writing the newly assigned number in the upper right corner of
each piece. To make a record of the new folder number, she
prepares a file card and puts it in its correct alphabetic place
in the card index file.

For example, if the correspondence of the Norwood Ap-
pliance Company, which is housed in the miscellaneous alphabetic file, becomes active enough to warrant the opening of an
individual folder, and if the number of the last folder in the
file is 462, the file clerk (1) removes the correspondence with

this company from the folder in the miscellaneous alphabetic file, (2) assigns number 463 to this correspondent by completing a file card, (3) erases the "M" code on each piece of correspondence and substitutes the numeric code "463" in the upper right corner, (4) files the file card alphabetically, and (5) files the correspondence in the numeric correspondence file by opening a new folder bearing the caption 463.

Terminal Digit System   Many serially numbered items, such as checks, letters of credit, mortgages, hospital case records, and insurance applications and policies, with numbers of five, six, and even seven digits, are troublesome to handle. The material carrying the highest numbers is the most active, and reference by several clerks simultaneously will be physically difficult because this material is housed in only a few drawers and the clerks get in each other's way. Distribution of work is difficult, and the long numbers slow down the operation.

In terminal-digit files, filing is done by the *final* digits. In a six-digit number such as 234,567, the digits could be separated in two ways. Separation of the digits into two-digit groups is shown below:

Primary	Secondary	Final
23	45	67

Separation of the digits into three-digit groups may be done as follows:

Primary	Final
234	567

Using the last example, within the file drawer allocated to the final or terminal 567, the item 234 567 would appear between 233 567 and 235 567.

Fewer errors occur with the use of this system, as the clerk is not required to hold the full number in her mind as she works. Material can be sorted faster, and time savings of 25 to 50 per cent have been realized by some companies.

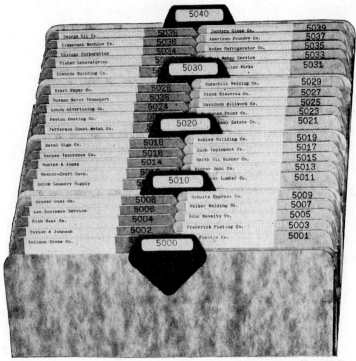

—*Shaw-Walker Co.*

Illustration 10H, Numeric-Name System

Numeric-Name System   In this system, made by the Shaw-Walker Company, numbers are printed on the folder tabs, which are wide enough to accommodate gummed labels indicating the name or subject of the folder. By showing both a number and a name, additional identity is given to each folder and makes filing and finding faster and surer. Another feature of this system is that even-numbered tabs are attached to the left side of the folders and odd-numbered tabs to the right side.

In Illustration 10H, notice that the arrangement is determined by the numeric sequence, not by the alphabetic sequence of names. Thus, the system is primarily numeric and indirect, requiring a supplementary alphabetic card file for indentification purposes.

QUESTIONS

1. What is a numeric file?

2. Under what circumstances may a numeric file be used profitably?

3. Of what three parts does a numeric correspondence file consist?

4. In a numeric file what bearing has the alphabetic order of names on the assigning of numbers to new correspondents?

5. In what order are letters filed in a numbered subject folder?

6. Describe the arrangement of the numeric file illustrated on page 96.

7. Explain the use of the supplementary card index file.

8. What is the purpose of the miscellaneous alphabetic file in a numeric filing system?

9. What is the purpose of an accession book?

10. To what does "preliminary name coding" refer?

11. What is the very first step in the numeric coding process?

12. Describe the entire numeric coding process.

13. How is a cross reference handled when all the correspondence to which the reference is made is filed in one folder?

14. How is a cross reference handled when related correspondence is filed in different folders?

15. Where and how are materials coded "M" filed?

16. In general, when is an individual folder added to a nunumeric file?

17. Describe the process of opening an individual folder.

18. How is a number read in terminal-digit filing.

PROBLEMS

1. Assume that a numeric file is to be made for the following list of names and in the order that they are listed. You may assume that the accession book indicates that the next number to use is 432. Assign a number to each name; then arrange the names in alphabetic order.

James A. Berry Sons Co., Inc.
States Service Oil Corp.
Richard F. Hobson Petroleum
  Corp.
Kleen Heat Petroleum Corp.
Original Consumers Oil Fuel
  Co.

Irwin J. Richards Fuel Co.
All-Boro Fuel Corp.
Landi Bros. Coal Concern
Town & Country Oil Corp.
Dale-Finley Oil Corp.

Wilson & Company Oil Products
Overseas Oil and Petroleum
  Co.
P. R. Atlas Fuel Co.
Petro Fuel Oil Corp.
Fenway & Morris Coal & Oil
  Co.

Madison Heating Corp.
Sta-Neet Oil Heating Company
Sidney B. Lowelson & Sons
T. H. Taylor & Sons
OK Coal Supply Company

Burnside Coal Co., Inc.
National Fuel Terminals
Globe Heating Corp.
  Dover, New Jersey
Kirk's Fuel & Oil
Extra-Safe Oil Heating Co.

Hi-Flame Coal & Fuel Oil
  Corp.
Ajax Petroleum Corp.
Charlie's Central Petroleum
  Corp.
John H. Ferris Oil Heating
  Co.
Lowell-Freeman Coal Co.

Globe Heating Corp.
  Hillsdale, New Jersey
Wonderful Oil Corp. of
  America
Black-Tillman Refining Corp.
S G Coal & Oil Fuel Service

Diamond Oil Supplies
The Olinville Oil Supply Co.
E & J Petroleum Products
Rite-U-R Oil Products
Midtown Fuel Service, Inc.

Arman-Duncan Oil and Fuel Co.
Certified Petroleum Corp.
James V. Powers Refining Co.
A. James Hill Refining Corp.
Harold Lee White Oil
  Corporation

Liberty Fuel Company
The Safety Oil Corporation
Rodney J. De Marco Fuel, Inc.
Hudson Fuel Corporation
Nathan-Strong Fuel Corp.

S. T. Kellogg Refining Co.

2. As in Problem 1, assign a number to each of the following
   names beginning with 165 and then arrange the names in
   alphabetic order.

A. N. Braddock Mat Service
Anthony Edwards-Mason Rubber
  Mfg.
Herbert Jarman Rubber
  Products
Henrite Products Corporation
Lord-Henson Crude Rubber
  Corp.

New Hampshire Mechanical
  Rubber Co.
George Oliver Fulton Rubber
  Products
Aborne Rubber Company
I. William Keaton Rubber
  Manufacturers
O'Sullivan Rubber Corp.

Ideal Rubber Products
  Adams, Pennsylvania
Victoria Rubber Mfg. Co.
Christopher Edwards & Sons
The Miller Rubber Sales
  Company

Rubberhide Company
Martin B. Gordon Rawhide
  Products
P & G Davol Rubber Products
Ideal Rubber Products
  Adams, Nebraska

(*This problem is completed on
the next page.*)

Jacob P. Prescott Rubber & Sponge
T. O. Smithers & Company
London-Johnson Rubber & Plastics
United Cities Rubber Mechanical Goods
Minnesota Injection Molded Rubber

Hewitt-Robbins Rubber Products

H. O. Canfield Rubber Corporation
Cardinal-Keyes Rubber Suction Cups
Robert F. Von Huston Belting Products
Admiral Foam Rubber Co.
Graton & Knight Products Corp.

O & P Rubber Company
Thermoid Rubber Tubing Co.
R R Rubber Supply Company
W. E. Williams' Rubber Products
Keaton Rubber Company

A B C House of Rubber Goods
McCormick & Boyle Rubber Tubing
Stowe-Wilkins Rubber Mfg. Co.
O. W. Jackson & Company
Sav-A-Top Rubber Magic, Inc.

U R Rubber Manufacturers
National Rubber & Plastic Mfg. Co.
Phillip Roger Brenner Rubber Corp.
Tyer Rubber Company
Milton J. Owens & Co.

Voorhees Rubber Mfg. Co., Inc.
P R & Y Rubber Specialty Company
Peter J. Henry Rubber Supplies
Sponge Rubber Products
George Leslie Fulton Rubber Products

The Dayton Rubber Company

JOB 6—NUMERIC CORRESPONDENCE FILING

At this time complete Job 6 in FILING OFFICE PRAC-TICE, Second Edition. The instructions and supplies for this job are included in the practice set.

Chapter 11

SUBJECT FILING

Direct Subject Filing

Nature of Subject Filing A subject file is one in which the divisions of the file, as indicated by the guide captions, are based upon subjects. The subject titles may correspond to those that make up an alphabetically arranged outline of the activities, the departments, or the problems of a business or an office. For example, a subject filing system might be based upon the following alphabetic list of activities or departments in a business:

Accounting	Personnel
Administration	Production
Credit	Purchasing
Filing	Sales
Orders	Shipping

Each one of the foregoing subject headings would probably be subdivided. For example, the subject divisions for the Sales Department might be:

Advertising	Customers
Branch Offices	Exhibits
Conferences	Salesmen

Subject subdivisions might also be necessary for each of the subject divisions. For example, the Advertising division of the Sales Department section of the file might include these subdivisions:

Direct-Mail
Magazines
Newspapers

Uses of Subject Filing Subject filing can be used to advantage whenever it is desirable to have correspondence pertaining to one subject grouped in one place in the files, or whenever the subjects to which correspondence is related are more important than the names of the correspondents. This situation is more frequently true of single departments in a business than it is for a centralized file for an entire business. The correspondence of one department is usually related to a relatively small number of subjects with few divisions and subdivisions, which fit into a simple classification that everyone in the department who has occasion to use the file understands thoroughly.

Unless the business is very small, the correspondence that is handled by a central filing department relates to so many different subjects, some of which overlap, that it is difficult for the file clerk to determine the subject code for each letter and to remember that subject when the letter is requested later without reference to its subject code. For this reason centralized files usually incorporate the necessary subject folders in a basic alphabetic system similar to the type described in Chapter 5.

When subject filing is used in a central filing department, all customer material is filed by the name of the customer, but all matters dealing with the operation of the business are filed by subject according to a classification that has been designed to meet the needs of the business. The subject file brings together all material on Advertising, Sales, Personnel, Taxes, Insurance, Office Procedures, etc. This material is usually kept longer than customer material, and segregating it into a subject file gives it the protection it warrants.

Other examples of the principles involved in subject filing are entries in an index in a book and lists of equipment in a catalog.

Arrangement of a Subject File The guides in a subject file may appear in one, two, or three positions, depending upon the number of headings, divisions, and subdivisions in the outline of subjects involved in the correspondence. For example, primary guides might be used in first position to indicate the subjects representing the main headings of the outline; auxiliary guides might appear in second position to represent the divisions of each main heading in the outline. If the division headings in the outline are in turn subdivided, guides in a third position could carry such captions.

All folders in a file may be of one type with captions consisting of subject headings only, or a filing system may include folders of a second type for names of individuals and businesses. There is no miscellaneous folder in a subject file to compare with that in an alphabetic file. Each letter is classified according to its content.

In the following illustration of a portion of a subject file drawer, the primary guides in first position indicate the main

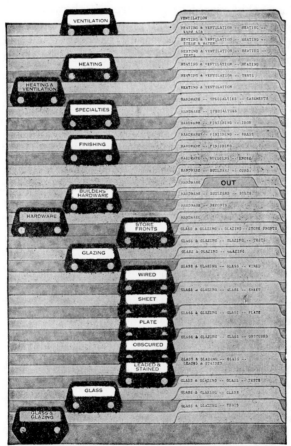

—*Automatic File & Index Co.*

Illustration 11A, Subject File

headings of the subject outline. Following the first guide, "Glass and Glazing," are the captions of the two auxiliary guides for this section of the file in second position. The first of these auxiliary guides, with the caption "Glass," is further divided by the captions on the five guides in third position. There is a double-width folder in last position, following each of the guides. In actual practice each of the guides would be followed by several folders rather than just one. The purpose of the illustration is to indicate the arrangement of the guides and folders in a relatively small space, and therefore all of the folders that would be used are not shown.

When folders for individual correspondents are included in a subject file, some auxiliary guides with alphabetic captions may be necessary in addition to the guides with subject captions.

Subject Filing Procedure   In using a subject file, the file clerk must be familiar with the following procedure:

Inspection. Each incoming letter should be checked to see that it has been released for filing.

Coding. In many cases the correspondence is coded by an executive or his secretary before it is sent to the filing department. If a letter has not been coded in this manner, the file clerk must read it carefully to determine the subject classification to be used as a basis for coding. If the subject appears in the letter in a form identical with that on the caption of the folder in which the letter should be filed, the coding may be done by underscoring the subject wherever it appears in the letter. In most cases, however, it is necessary to code the letter by writing the subject classification at the top of the letter or in the upper right-hand corner.

To prevent errors in coding, a master record of the subject captions and the kinds of correspondence filed in each of the folders bearing these captions should be available at all times in the filing department. This master record may be in the form of a typewritten outline with explanatory comments, in the form of a card index file with all subject captions arranged alphabetically, or in both forms. Unless some type of supplementary record is kept, two file clerks may use two different subjects for coding letters of the same type. More differences of opinion arise regarding the coding of letters for a subject file than for any other type of file. Thus, in addition to using a master record, it is also advisable to have one person take responsibility for making final decisions on subject coding problems.

Cross References. A cross-reference sheet should be prepared if more than one subject is involved in the same piece of correspondence. In the illustration on page 112 the information on the cross-reference sheet indicates (1) that a letter from the Adams Drugstore requested two things, information concerning office desks and an extension of credit, (2) that the letter was filed in a folder bearing the caption "Information (Requests for)—Office Desks," and (3) that the cross-reference sheet should be filed in the "Credit (Requests for)" folder so that anyone who looks in that folder for the correspondence with the Adams Drugstore will know that he should look also in the other folder.

Sorting. After all material has been coded, it should be sorted first according to the main subjects of the file and second by the first divisions. This means that if the file is based upon an outline consisting of five main headings, the first sorting would be on the basis of such headings. For each of these sorted groups the second sorting would be based upon the divisions for the main heading in the outline.

Placing Material in Folders. Material in a subject folder should be arranged first by the alphabetic order of subjects if more than one subject is involved. The first basis for arrangement of materials in a single subject folder, however, is the alphabetic order of the names of the correspondents so that all correspondence with one person or company is grouped together in the folder. Different pieces of correspondence for the same correspondent are arranged within that group by date, with the latest date in front. Material that is placed in an individual folder is arranged in the same manner as that in an individual folder for an alphabetic name file, that is, the latest date in front.

CROSS-REFERENCE SHEET

Name or Subject _Credit (Requests for)_
Adams Drugstore
Minneapolis 3, Minnesota
Date of Item _March 5, 19--_

Regarding

SEE

Name or Subject _Information (Requests for)_
Office Desks

Authorized by _Claire Maddox_ Date _March 10, 19--_

Illustration 11B, Cross-Reference Sheet for a Subject File

Index to   Since material in a subject file is arranged by
Subject File   subject, an index of the subject headings and
subdivisions under the main headings and of
the cross references is necessary. A card index covering the
subjects set up in a file helps file clerks to be more consistent
in the use of the same subject in coding letters of the same
type. In the same index all names of correspondents are
placed in their proper alphabetic order.

Subject System for   As mentioned on page 108, the subject
Departmental Files   system can be used to advantage in a
relatively small departmental file. In
such a situation the indexing plan for the system is based
upon an outline of major and minor departmental operations
and functions. The outline, when translated into a guiding
system for the subject file, will show major departmental
functions as titles for primary guides. Subdivisions of functions will be used for notations on secondary guides.

The departmental or operational subject system is illustrated by the executive file shown on page 114. Guides in first
position (1) are marked to show the three major functions—
Corporation Matters, Equipment and Supplies, and Finance
and Accounting. Each of these major sections is divided by
secondary guides (2), which show titles for principal phases
in each section. Miscellaneous folders (3) are used for subjects having only a few papers. Individual folders (4) and
(5) are provided for materials of particular importance, and
special guides (6) are used to show very active or very important sections in the file.

This plan for an executive file can be adapted for use in
other departments or areas of operation, provided that the
headings in the outline of departmental functions are concise
and distinctive.

In preparing to use such a system as that shown in Illustration 11C, page 114, utmost care should be exercised to insure
that divisions in the system reflect the major and minor functions of a particular department. An analysis of departmental
functions as they relate to filing requirements should be made
by those most familiar with them.

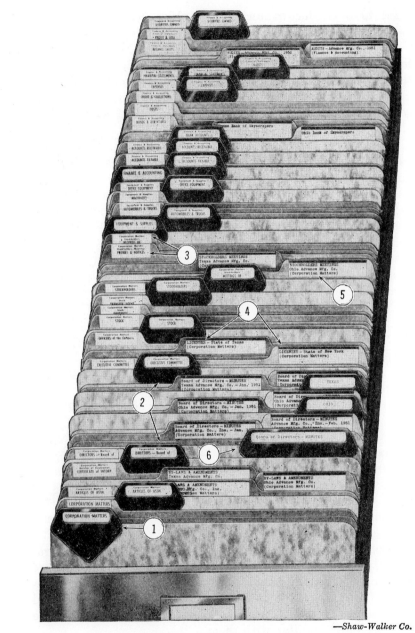

—*Shaw-Walker Co.*

Illustration 11C, Executive File

Use of Numbers and Letters in Subject File Notations

Subject Numeric File   Numbered notations on guide and folder tabs may be used in subject correspondence files just as they are used in alphabetic name files, as follows:

1. As a part of the subject captions to facilitate filing. Subject titles are frequently quite long and seldom appear in their exact form in correspondence. Considerable time can be saved, therefore, if numbers instead of words are used in coding and in locating folders in the files.

2. As a substitute for subject captions. When only numbers are used for captions, then subject headings, divisions, or subdivisions that are closely related can be grouped together in the files even though the subject titles do not fall in the same alphabetic section. When this plan is followed, a supplementary card index file, arranged alphabetically by subjects, is necessary and is used in a manner similar to that for numeric correspondence files. This is an indirect method of filing, however, and is not commonly used.

The simplest type of numbering is that used in the following example, in which the subject titles are the same as those used in the first pages of this chapter.

Number	Heading	Division	Subdivision
100	Accounting		
200	Administration		
300	Credit		
400	Filing		
500	Orders		
600	Production		
700	Purchasing		
800	Sales		
810		Advertising	
811			Direct-Mail
812			Magazines
813			Newspapers
820		Branch Offices	
830		Conferences	
840		Customers	
850		Exhibits	
860		Salesmen	
900	Shipping		

Subject Decimal   A simple numbering system is adequate
Filing   for most subject files. When the outline
                       upon which a subject filing system is based
is more complicated or detailed, however, a decimal system
can be used to advantage.

Perhaps the most widely known and used decimal system
is that devised by Melvil Dewey. It is used by libraries to
classify books, catalogues, pamphlets, and all related materials. Dewey's system divides all human knowledge into nine
main groups and one general group. The arrangement of
numbers and subjects is as follows:

000	General Works	500	Natural Science
100	Philosophy	600	Useful Arts
200	Religion	700	Fine Arts
300	Sociology	800	Literature
400	Philology	900	History

These major groups, in turn, are divided into nine subdivisions and one general division. For example, the "Useful
Arts (600)" section has these subdivisions:

600	General
610	Medicine
620	Engineering
630	Agriculture
640	Domestic Economy
650	Commerce
660	Chemical Technology
670	Manufactures
680	Mechanical Trades
690	Building Trades

These sections are further subdivided into groups of ten.
Then, by the use of decimals, the subdivisions can be continued indefinitely.

Use of Decimal   The Dewey Decimal System, or some
Systems to Classify   adaptation of this system, can be em-
Business Records   ployed to advantage in business filing
                           when provision for expansion in the
files must be made and when detailed subdivisions in a filing
system are needed. To be efficient, such filing systems must
be carefully organized and the file operators must be thoroughly familiar with the subject outline upon which the

system is based. Many railroads use a variation of the Dewey system called the Williams Decimal System, which groups and numbers the principal types of railroad activities into major and minor divisions.

Direct Subject Filing—Decimal The principal advantages of the direct decimal-subject system over the alphabetic system for certain kinds of materials are illustrated by the Yawman and Erbe direct subject filing system shown below. Notice that all related materials are grouped in one place in the file, that a section can be expanded without sacrificing orderly identification (Section 705), and that the decimal numbers may be identified with specific items (e.g. numbered stock items) or related to accounting or auditing classifications.

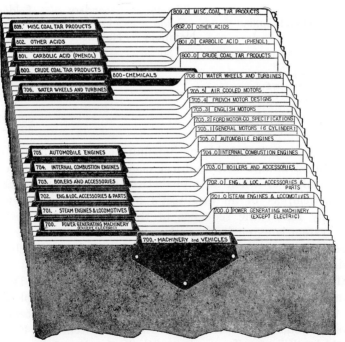

—*Yawman and Erbe Mfg. Co.*

Illustration 11D, Direct Subject Filing—Decimal

Armed Forces Decimal Filing The basic filing system of the Armed Forces, as described in *War Department Decimal File System* and *Navy Filing Manual,* is adapted from the Dewey Decimal System. The classification of the topics in the correspondence records and reports of the Armed Forces is based upon the following main groups:

000	General	500	Transportation
100	Finance and Accounting	600	Buildings and Grounds
200	Personnel	700	Medicine, Hygiene, and
300	Administration		Sanitation
400	Supplies, Equipment, and Services	800	Rivers, Harbors, and Waterways

Other Captions for Subject Files Several other systems for subject caption notations are less commonly used. The first of these is known as Duplex-Numeric. The following example indicates the general nature and use of the system.

Subject Outline	Primary Guide Notations	Secondary Guide Notations	Folder Notations
Office Maintenance Expense	30		
Typewriters		30-1	
Royal			30-1-1
Underwood			30-1-2
L C Smith			30-1-3
Filing Equipment		30-2	
Legal Files			30-2-1
Solid Cabinets			30-2-2

This system is capable of indefinite expansion and can be used to advantage when subject classifications are numerous and detailed or when an alphabetical arrangement would be impractical, as in an architect's office, where a file would logically follow the sequence of the erection of a building. The system is extensively used in law offices, where the client is assigned a number, and every case handled for the client is assigned an auxiliary number of the client's number.

If letters are substituted for numbers in the Duplex-Numeric system, the method is known as Duplex-Alphabetic. In the example used for the Duplex-Numeric system, the duplex-alphabetic caption for Office Maintenance Expense would be "C"; for Typewriters "C-a"; for Royal typewriters "C-a-a."

Another system, the Alpha-Numeric, is a combination of the two preceding systems in that capital letters are used for the main headings of the outline; numbers are used for the first divisions of the main headings; and small letters are used for the subject subdivisions. In other words, letters and numbers are used alternately to determine the caption notations.

Illustration 11E, on page 120, indicates the application of five different systems of coding the same items in a subject outline. Notice that some of the coding systems are not adapted to the subject outline given in the first column. The simple numeric outline is not adequate, and some of the duplex outlines appear unwieldy. However, these systems are very useful in certain situations. For example, the simple numeric is useful in correspondence filing, and the duplex systems are used to advantage in marking or noting stock items, scientific data, and the like.

QUESTIONS

1. What is a subject file?
2. When is it advantageous to use a subject file?
3. Describe one possible arrangement for a subject file.
4. What types of folders may be used in a subject file?
5. What is the purpose of the master record of the subject captions and the kinds of correspondence filed in each of the folders?
6. When should a cross-reference sheet be prepared?
7. After materials have been coded, how should they be sorted?
8. How are materials placed in folders?
9. What is a subject numeric file?
10. How are numbered notations on guide and folder tabs used?
11. What is a subject decimal file?
12. Give an example of the use of the Dewey Decimal System.
13. What is the Williams Decimal System?
14. Describe the general nature of the Duplex-Numeric System.
15. In what way is the Duplex-Alphabetic System similar to the Duplex-Numeric System?
16. What is the Alpha-Numeric System?

SUBJECTS AND SUBDIVISIONS	SIMPLE NUMERIC	DECIMAL	DUPLEX-NUMERIC	DUPLEX-ALPHABETIC	ALPHA-NUMERIC
ADVERTISING	100	100.	10	A	A
Rates	110	110.	10-1	A-a	A-1
Magazine	111	111.	10-1-1	A-a-a	A-1-a
Newspaper	112	112.	10-1-2	A-a-b	A-1-b
Outdoor	113	113.	10-1-3	A-a-c	A-1-c
Copy	120	120.	10-2	A-b	A-2
Magazine	121	121.	10-2-1	A-b-a	A-2-a
American	*No numbers are available for these items*	121.1	10-2-1-1	A-b-a-a	A-2-a-1
January		121.11	10-2-1-1-1	A-b-a-a-a	A-2-a-1-a
February		121.12	10-2-1-1-2	A-b-a-a-b	A-2-a-1-b
Time		121.2	10-2-1-2	A-b-a-b	A-2-a-2
January		121.21	10-2-1-2-1	A-b-a-b-a	A-2-a-2-a
February		121.22	10-2-1-2-2	A-b-a-b-b	A-2-a-2-b
OFFICE MAINTENANCE	200	200.	20	B	B
Typewriters	210	210.	20-1	B-a	B-1

Illustration 11E, A Comparison of the Various Notations Used in Subject Filing

PROBLEMS

1. Distribute the following items under the headings that
   are presented and then arrange the headings and each
   item under its proper heading in alphabetic order.

Mining
Manufacturing
Finance & Insurance
Services

Transportation
Communication & Public Utilities
Government & Government Enterprises

Finances
Security, commodity, & ex-
   change brokers
Leather products manufactures
Rubber goods manufactures
Non-metallic mining

Stone, clay & glass manu-
   factures
Anthracite mining
Legal services
Bus lines
Gold mining

Health services
Radio broadcasting
Bauxite mining
Paper & paper products
   manufactures
Local government enterprises

Federal government enter-
   prises
Freight trains
Copper mining
Passenger trains
Gas

Telephone & telegraph
Educational services
Bituminous mining
Business services
Pipe-line transportation

Hotels & lodging places
Personal services
Furniture products, manufac-
   ture of
Air transportation
Railroads

Tobacco manufactures
Silver mining
State government enterprises
Employment agencies
Textile manufactured products

Insurance carriers
Engineering services
Chemical products, manufac-
   ture of
Automobiles & equipment
   manufactures

Water transportation
Insurance
Electricity
Banking
Electrical machinery, manu-
   facture of

Petroleum & natural gas,
   mining of

2. The following list of items are produced or used on farms.
   The headings to be used are listed below. Arrange both
   the headings and each item under its proper heading in
   alphabetic order.

Livestock
Field Crops
Fruits

Vegetables
Livestock Products
Nuts

Grapefruit	Beans
Soybeans	Eggs
Oranges	Potatoes
Corn for grain	Grapes
Alfalfa	Walnuts
Butter	Meat and Lard
Hay	Mules and Mule Colts
Oats	Plums and Prunes
Cotton	Corn
Peaches	Hogs and Pigs
Cheese	Almonds
Wheat	Sheep and Lambs
Pears	Cherries
Rice	Horses and Colts
Chickens	Milk
Turkeys	Tomatoes
Cattle & Calves	Barley
Pecans	Tobacco
Beets	Flax
Peas	Cows
Cabbage	Sugar cane

JOB 7—SUBJECT FILING PRACTICE

At this time complete Job 7 in FILING OFFICE PRAC-
TICE, Second Edition. The instructions and supplies for
this job are included in the practice set.

JOB 8—DECIMAL, DUPLEX-NUMERIC, DUPLEX-ALPHABETIC, AND ALPHA-NUMERIC CODES

At this time complete Job 8 in FILING OFFICE PRAC-
TICE, Second Edition. The instructions and supplies for
this job are included in the practice set.

Chapter · 12

· GEOGRAPHIC FILING

Nature and Uses of Geographic filing is an alphabetic
Geographic Filing method based primarily upon the geographic locations of correspondents.
Files of this type may be based upon an alphabetic arrangement of states or territories, cities, and names of persons and
businesses for correspondence that is national in scope; of
cities and names for correspondence limited to one state;
or of districts, streets, and names for local correspondence.

The exact organization that is used in a geographic filing
system depends upon the geographical districts in which the
correspondents are located, the type of business, and the use
that is made of the filed material.

The geographic filing method has distinct advantages for
those businesses which classify their records by geographic
districts. Since the work in sales departments is frequently
organized by geographic areas, correspondence files organized
on the same basis make it possible to check, control, analyze,
and summarize the activities of the departments more efficiently. Mail-order houses, publishing companies, steamship
lines, and large wholesale houses are only a few of the types
of businesses that find it advantageous to use the geographic
filing method.

Arrangement of a In a geographic correspondence file pri-
Geographic File mary guides are usually reserved for the
names of the largest geographic divisions
involved, for example, names of states. Auxiliary guides are
used for the remaining geographic divisions, as well as the
alphabetic sections into which any one of the geographic units
might be subdivided. Folders may be used for miscellaneous
state correspondence, miscellaneous city correspondence, and
the correspondence of individuals or businesses. The miscellaneous state and city folders may bear only geographic names
if the correspondence for each state or city is not great

enough to justify alphabetic divisions. If alphabetic break-
downs are necessary, as is frequently true in the case of
larger states and cities, the miscellaneous folders bear alphabetic notations.

Illustration 12A shows a geographic filing system in which
the primary unit is a state name (Ohio) that is indicated by
a guide in central position. Secondary guides in this system
show names of cities and follow the state guide in positions 1,
2, and 3. Fourth position is reserved for special sections and
fifth position is used for individual and miscellaneous folders.

Notice that two varieties of special sections are shown in
fourth position: (1) an alphabetic breakdown behind the
Cincinnati guide, and (2) a chronological breakdown following the name of a company (the Brooks Co.) located in Cleveland. Both sections in fourth position indicate that the volume
of correspondence has been sufficient to warrant the inclusion
of additional guides and folders to relieve the congestion that
would otherwise occur in the parts of the system. Notice also
that OUT guides are cut to show in fourth position.

In this particular geographic filing system, all folders are
placed in the extreme right-hand position (fifth) and are used
in two different ways: (1) The majority of these folders are
used for individual and firm names—the geographic location
being written first followed by the name of the person or firm.
(2) Miscellaneous folders for cities are also placed in fifth
position and are given distinctively colored labels. Miscellaneous folders for cities are not automatically included in
this system and are not added until required. In other words,
filing is directed toward establishing individual folders as soon
as possible and keeping miscellaneous filing to a minimum.
There are many variations in the guiding systems used for
geographic filing. For example, in comparison with the plan
shown in Illustration 12A, other plans use alphabetic guides
in place of city name guides; others provide a miscellaneous
folder for each city or for each alphabetic section included
in the system. Regardless of the guiding plan used, however,
the geographic location of correspondents is used as the primary coding unit and all materials are considered first on
this basis.

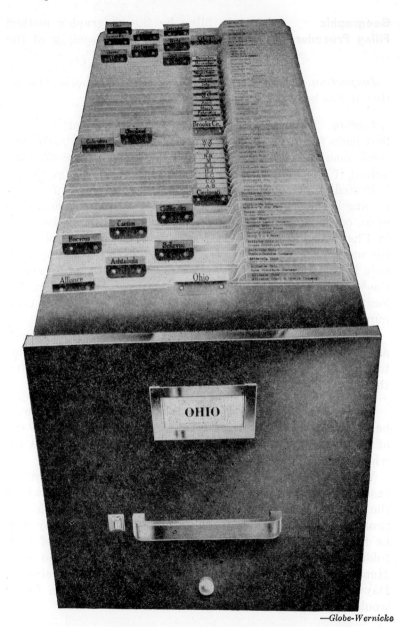

—*Globe-Wernicke*

Illustration 12A, Geographic File

Geographic Accurate filing by the geographic method
Filing Procedure requires a thorough understanding of the
following steps.

Inspection. Each incoming letter should be checked to see
that it has been released for filing.

Coding. Inasmuch as geographic locations constitute the
first basis for filing correspondence by this method, such locations should be clearly marked. This is the only coding required if the name of the individual or business is clearly
indicated in the letterhead, heading, or signature of an incoming letter, or as a part of the inside address on the carbon
of an outgoing letter. Quite frequently, however, as indicated
in Chapter 6 on alphabetic correspondence filing procedure,
the name under which a communication is to be filed appears
only in the body of the letter or is not indicated anywhere in
the letter. In such cases the name, as well as the geographic
location, should be marked or written at the top of the communication.

Since some letters require the marking of the name as well
as the geographic location, a desirable coding procedure seems
to be that of encircling the geographic title and underscoring
the individual or firm name.

Cross References. Cross references in a geographic file may
be of two types: (1) cross references, indicated by the use
of visible cross-reference cards, and (2) cross-references for
which cross-reference sheets are used.

Visible cross-reference cards are used, for example, in the
case of a company having branches in several cities, where
the correspondence in one folder will frequently pertain to
problems and conditions in the other offices. This may also
be handled by a "See also" label on the front flap of each
folder, referring to the other folders. For example, the Ajax
Manufacturing Company has offices in Canton, Cincinnati,
Dayton, and Toledo. On the front flap of the Canton folder
would appear a label reading:

See also:　Cincinnati, Dayton, Toledo

CROSS-REFERENCE SHEET

Name or Subject _Arizona, Phoenix_
Hanna – Holt Hardware Store

Date of Item _May 20, 19——_

Regarding _Hardware Dealers Convention_

SEE

Name or Subject _Colorado, Denver_
Mountain States Hardware Co.

Authorized by _Claire Maddox_ Date _May 25, 19——_

Illustration 12B, Cross-Reference Sheet for a Geographic File

Sorting. Letters are sorted by geographic units, starting with the largest for the first sorting and continuing until all the units involved in the filing system have been used. For example, the first sorting might be on the basis of states, and the second sorting on the basis of cities or towns.

Placing Material in Folders. The first step in placement of materials in their proper folders is the location of the folder for each item. The file clerk locates the proper file drawer by reading the drawer labels, and then finds in that drawer the section for the proper state. She uses the auxiliary guides for the purpose of locating the proper city section. Usually this is as far as the guides can be used in locating folders.

The next step for the file clerk is to examine the folders in the city section to determine whether or not an individual folder exists for the correspondent. If there is such a folder, the communication is filed in it in the same manner that a communication would be placed in an individual folder in an alphabetic file.

If there is no individual folder, the file clerk places the communication in a miscellaneous city folder if there is one. Here letters are grouped first in alphabetic order by correspondents' names and then in each group by date. If there is no city folder, the communication is placed in the miscellaneous state alphabetic folder in which the correspondence is grouped first by city or town, then in each city group by names of correspondents, and finally in each correspondents' group by date.

Card Index File   Cross reference from individual to location is possible only when a card index is maintained. Such a card index file, arranged alphabetically by names of correspondents, is frequently used to supplement a geographic file because problems arise when individuals who request correspondence from the files do not remember the geographic location of the correspondent, or when a correspondent changes his address or writes from a location other than his business address. Since it is desirable to keep all material of a customer in one folder, this supplemental index can prove invaluable in the use of a geographic system. If, when material is filed, the file clerk finds no previous correspondence for a name, she can then check the supplementary index. If the name is a new one, she can add a card for it to the index and prepare a folder.

Subject Filing in a Geographic System   Certain correspondence pertaining to special subjects, such as applications, can be filed to advantage in any system by using special subject folders. In a geographic system the difficulty encountered is that of giving a geographic location to correspondence which is related because of its subject matter but which involves a number of different geographic locations. The best solution for this problem seems to be that of grouping all special subject folders in one part of the files separate from the ordinary correspondence. If it is considered desirable to maintain the geographic arrangement for all materials, regardless of type, the special subject folders can be arbitrarily assigned the geographic location of the business that maintains the filing system.

Geographic and Subject Filing in an Alphabetic System   Geographic as well as subject materials can be effectively handled in a system that is primarily alphabetic. This is accomplished in the Shaw-Walker system shown in Illustration 12C, page 130. The guiding system is alphabetic, with primary guides (1) in positions one and two marking the major divisions in the system. Miscellaneous folders (2) are provided for each alphabetic section just as they are in any regular alphabetic system. The third position is used for guides that mark special sections (3) by names, such as Pacific, Parker, and Peterson; by geographic locations, such as Pennsylvania and Philadelphia; or by subjects, such as Plastic. Miscellaneous folders (4) are also provided for each special section. Individual folders (5) are in third and fourth positions and special guides (6) of double width for very active records are marked with tabs in last position.

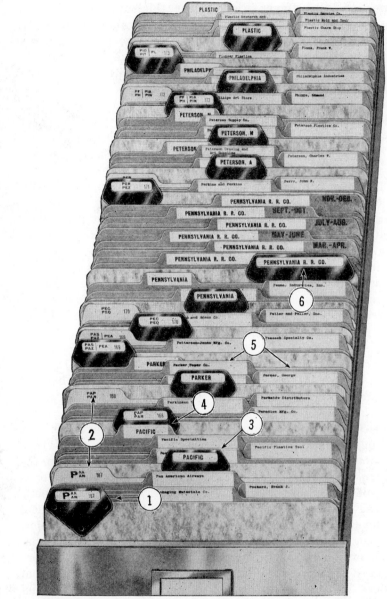

—Shaw-Walker Co.

Illustration 12C, Controlling Index

QUESTIONS

1. What is a geographic file?
2. Upon what factors does the exact organization of a geographic filing system depend?
3. Name a few of the types of businesses that use the geographic filing method.
4. Describe one possible arrangement for a geographic file.
5. Explain coding procedure in a geographic file.
6. What two types of cross references are used in a geographic file?
7. How are letters sorted after they have been coded geographically?
8. How are letters filed in miscellaneous city folders?
9. How are letters filed in miscellaneous alphabetic section folders?
10. For what purpose is a card index file used in a geographic filing system?
11. How is correspondence pertaining to special subjects handled?

PROBLEMS

1. Arrange the following list of names according to state and then according to city or town within the state.

Jewel Food Center
Roseburg, Oregon

Hi-Ho Food Center
Bristol, Rhode Island

Manville Grocery Store
Saluda, South Carolina

Imperial Grocery Store
Aiken, South Carolina

Kanes's Food Center
Antlers, Oklahoma

Harold's Dairy & Food Center
Newport, Rhode Island

Indian Point Food Center
Columbia, South Carolina

Michael's Grocery
Newkirk, Oklahoma

Hillside Grocery
Hillsboro, Oregon

Lafayette Food Center
Newberry, South Carolina

Kopper Grocery
Dillon, South Carolina

Lancaster Grocery
Astoria, Oregon

Kanes' Grocery
Bellefont, Pennsylvania

Majestic Grocery & Dairy
Fossil, Oregon

Jefferson's Food Shop
Clearfield, Pennsylvania

Master Dairy
East Greenwich, Rhode Island

High View Food Center
Pittsburgh, Pennsylvania

Jones' Food Center
Alva, Oklahoma

Lenox Grocery
Canyon City, Oregon

Hampton Grocery
Millford, Pennsylvania

Harris Food Store
Bamberg, South Carolina

Krandall Dairy & Grocery
  Store
Lock Haven, Pennsylvania

Hamilton Food Market
Moro, Oregon

Ideal Food Center
Pottsville, Pennsylvania

Jefferson Grocery & Dairy
Chester, South Carolina

Hightower Food Store
Laporte, Pennsylvania

Hygrade Grocery
Perry, Oklahoma

Highland Grocery
Clarion, Pennsylvania

Kenneth's Food Center
Cordell, Oklahoma

Island City Grocery
Ada, Oklahoma

Linden Grocery
Barnwell, South Carolina

Loyalty Food Center
Purcell, Oklahoma

Kraft Grocery
Providence, Rhode Island

Liberty Food Center
Baker, Oregon

Joel's Grocery Store
Easton, Pennsylvania

Home Service Food Market
Pawnee, Oklahoma

Lincoln Food Store
Reading, Pennsylvania

King's Dairy & Grocery Store
Mercer, Pennsylvania

Majestic Grocery
Charleston, South Carolina

Hudson Food Store
Altus, Oklahoma

King Cole Grocery
Abbeville, South Carolina

Hamilton Food Market
Butler, Pennsylvania

Jersey Food Center
Emporium, Pennsylvania

Jay's Self-Service Grocery
West Kingston, Rhode Island

Madison Grocery Store
Camden, South Carolina

Hilltop Grocery
Conway, South Carolina

Hunter Grocery
Oregon City, Oregon

Johnson's Food Store
Stillwater, Oklahoma

High City Food Center
Warren, Pennsylvania

Holly Grocery Store
Vale, Oregon

2. Arrange the following list of names according to the names of the states in the address and then according to cities.

T. S. Southern
5439 Folsom Avenue
Allen, Ohio

Miss Patricia Parker
192 Edgecombe Avenue
Clinton, Ohio

Mr. R. R. Rivers
522 Columbia Street
Hillsboro, New Hampshire

Mrs. Pauline Tropper
62 East Street
Ossipee, New Hampshire

Universal Motion Pictures
1000 Crown Place
Newport, New Hampshire

The E Z Woodworking Company
500 Boulevard Street
Keene, New Hampshire

Mrs. Martha P. Southland
408 Warren Street
Madison, Illinois

Wonder Chair Company
1788 Rose Street
Keene, New Hampshire

Bard-Norway Clothing Company
709 Arlington Avenue
Ashland, Ohio

The Banner Braid Company
23 Front Street
Ossipee, New Hampshire

Ross-Peterson, Inc.
1088 Fort Wayne Avenue
Clark, Ohio

Mrs. P. Wooster
5939 Williams Street
Clark, Ohio

Wyatt Brown, Incorporated
47 Garrison Street
Sullivan, New Hampshire

Sandy's Homes, Inc.
177 Carton Place
Edwards, Illinois

Master Raymond Thornby
100 Webster Road
Monroe, Ohio

Mr. Wallace C. Ford
57 Rolls Street
Grafton, New Hampshire

R. Arthur Pierpont
10 Ozone Street
Adams, Illinois

Mrs. Paul Wooster
458 Merrimack Road
Merrimack, New Hampshire

The American Slipper Company
56 Washington Boulevard
Crawford, Ohio

Mrs. Bertha Ross
16 Nye Street
Ossipee, New Hampshire

The State Savings Bank
10 Willow Street
Adams, Ohio

Mr. R. A. Pierpont
1003 Sands Street
Effingham, Illinois

The Wm. P. Green Typewriting
  Co.
930 East Street
Edwards, Illinois

Stan-Li Furniture Company
594 Lexington Avenue
Noble, Ohio

The No-Mar Express Company
459 Birmingham Ramp
Cheshire, New Hampshire

Bernard Manufacturing Company
494 Stone Place
Belknap, New Hampshire

National Tie Clip Company
23 Fourth Avenue
Clermont, Ohio

Sandy's Bar-B-Q Lunch
79 Grammar Street
Allen, Ohio

The Wm. P. Green Typewriting
    Co.
594 Haven Street
Effingham, Illinois

The Fast Ruler Company
18 Baskett Street
Clark, Ohio

Banster & Smith Fencing
    Company
55 Chrystie Street
Ossipee, New Hampshire

Empire Fastener Corporation
115 Western Street
Monroe, Illinois

B & M Motor Car Company
10 South River Street
Madison, Ohio

Weston Laboratory Supplies,
    Inc.
32 Dean Street
Macon, Illinois

Mrs. Theresa Colfax
41 Park Row West
Wabash, Illinois

Bernard Manufacturing Company
1075 Stanton Place
Belknap, New Hampshire

The Mineral Wealth Corpora-
    tion
4677 Carson Terrace
Crawford, Illinois

Stillwell Manufactures
7654 Othello Street
Belmont, Ohio

N. B. Wilson
27-29 Axena Street
Keene, New Hampshire

Sandy's Studio
One Shiller Place
Edwards, Illinois

Stan-Li Furniture Company
1098 Lexington Street
Noble, Ohio

Mrs. T. Colfax
43 Row Street
Crawford, Illinois

Empire Fastener Corporation
41 Montgomery Avenue
Ossipee, New Hampshire

Sandy's Automat
14 Watson Place
Clinton, Illinois

Mrs. Mary Bread
Government Relations
16 Nye Street
Ossipee, New Hampshire

Sandy's Bar-B-Q Lunch
68 Fountain Lane
Edwards, Illinois

Asian Products, Inc.
Lexington St. & First Avenue
Noble, Ohio

Wilson, Bennett & Roland,
    Manufacturers
230 West View Road
Clark, Ohio

Samuel Perkins Merchandising
18 Worth Street
Sullivan, New Hampshire

Thompson & Rivers, Inc.
24 Rollins Drive
Belmont, Ohio

JOB 9—GEOGRAPHIC FILING PRACTICE

*At this time complete Job 9 in FILING OFFICE PRAC-
TICE, Second Edition. The instructions and supplies for
this job are included in the practice set.*

Chapter · 13

· FILING SPECIAL TYPES
· OF RECORDS

The preceding chapters have dealt almost exclusively with the problems of filing correspondence and cards. In Chapter I, however, it was pointed out that all varieties of papers, forms, and records of business activities and transactions can be filed. In this chapter, only a few of the numerous special types of files are described. Other types are described and illustrated in the catalogs that are published by manufacturers of filing equipment and supplies.

Catalogs Catalogs are referred to frequently in the purchasing department of a business organization. Therefore they must be kept in good order and up to date.

Catalogs may be kept in bookcases or with their "backs up" in a vertical file cabinet. Catalogs may be arranged or filed in several ways: (1) by firm name—with a supplementary card index file, listing in alphabetic order the items or subjects included in each catalog, (2) by number—with an alphabetic card file of firm names and the subjects included in each catalog, (3) by subject—with an alphabetic card index listing of firm names.

Cross references may be made in the catalog card index, just as they are made in any other card system, by listing on one card the places where related material can be found. An example of this in a subject or article card index for catalogs filed by firm name is the file card shown in Illustration 13A at the left.

TRANSFER CASES			
Firm	Address	Catalog Number	Pages
ART METAL CONSTRUC-TION COMPANY	Jamestown, New York	41	9-10
AUTOMATIC FILE & INDEX COMPANY	Chicago, Illinois	35	33
GENERAL FIREPROOF-ING COMPANY	Youngstown, Ohio	36A	34

Illustration 13A, File Card in a Subject Card Index for Catalogs

—*Globe-Wernicke*

Illustration 13B, Map and Plan Files

Blueprints, Drawings, and Maps Some materials such as blueprints, drawings, and maps present a difficult filing problem because of their unusual sizes. They are usually filed vertically (without folding, if possible) in specially designed cabinets. A number system of guiding is frequently used to mark sections of such files, since architects' and contractors' work is usually taken and completed in numbered units. In some instances a subject marking system for guides is useful for this kind of record keeping.

Clippings and Pamphlets Small pamphlets and clippings from periodicals are frequently needed as records or for reference purposes in the course of business activity. Clipping files are very common, of course, in offices of newspapers and magazines.

Such materials can be filed in a regular vertical cabinet if the materials have been mounted on sheets of cardboard or paper. Clippings and pamphlets also can be glued or affixed by gummed tape to the sides of a regular folder.

Legal Papers Specially constructed document files are still used in some offices to house legal documents. Documents are folded and inserted into Manila or cardboard pocket folders. Modern filing equipment is made with drawers large enough to hold legal material, without folding, in regular vertical filing position.

The filing system most frequently used for legal papers is numeric since law cases are taken and completed in numbered units and since a number system keeps the files more private. A supplementary card file that serves as an index of clients' names must be kept in conjunction with the numeric system for legal papers. Such an index may be kept in a vault or a locked drawer.

Filing of Electros   The most convenient method of filing electros or "cuts" is to place them in shallow drawers, numbered and carefully indexed by subject of the electro. These electros are usually mounted on blocks of wood. If unmounted, they may be filed in a vertical cabinet in heavy envelopes with a picture of the cut on the outside of the envelope.

Stencil Filing   Because duplicator stencils are difficult to handle and hard to identify when they are filed, they present a special filing problem. It is possible to purchase specially constructed vertical cabinets which hold stencils in a vertical position on hangers which are movable and detachable. When this equipment is used, it is also possible to use movable guide tabs which can be affixed to the tops of the stencil hangers. Since these tabs are constructed so that desired labels can be inserted in them, a guiding system can be planned to suit individual filing needs.

While it is possible, and sometimes advisable, to use a straight alphabetic system for stencil files, it is usually more advantageous to plan a combination system of primary subject guides and secondary numeric guides. Numeric notations may be written on stencil tops. If the subject headings are not too complicated, it will be found that less handling of stencils will be necessary than in a system which requires that every stencil be placed in proper alphabetic sequence. An auxiliary card index arranged in alphabetic order should be sufficient to determine the exact location of a particular stencil in the main file.

On page 138 is a partial outline of guides and notations for the stencil and alphabetic card index files of a school. The portion of the outline shown is for the English Department.

STENCIL FILE	CARD INDEX FILE
English Department (Primary guide)	English Department (Primary guide)
Plays (Secondary guide)	Plays (Secondary guide)
1 ⎰ Individual 2 ⎱ stencil 3 ⎱ notations	"All American" 3 ⎰ Individual cards "Barcelona" 1 ⎱ filed in alpha- "Silver Box" 2 ⎱ betic order
Poems (Secondary guide)	Poems (Secondary guide)
1 2	"America" 2 "Beyond" 1
Radio Scripts (Secondary guide)	Radio Scripts (Secondary guide)
1 2	"Our City" 1 "Science Today" 2

QUESTIONS

1. What are three common ways of filing catalogs?
2. Are blueprints, maps, clippings, and other such materials filed horizontally or vertically?
3. What type of filing system is most frequently used for filing legal papers?
4. Describe a satisfactory method that uses primary subject guides and secondary numeric guides in filing stencils.
5. Describe two methods for filing electros.

PROBLEMS

1. Plan the arrangement of a stencil file for your school. Make the arrangement by department and subjects taught in each department.
2. Clip from newspapers and magazines everything you can find in some subject that interests you, and paste the clippings to 8½ x 11 paper. Then arrange for filing, using a subject matter breakdown.

Chapter 14

CARD RECORD SYSTEMS

Importance of Card Record Systems Card records of one kind or another are used by almost every business and service organization. The types of records kept on cards vary from simple data, such as personal names, to complex data, such as records of manufacturing costs. Libraries, schools, governmental agencies, dentists, doctors, banks, hospitals, and scores of other business and service firms, individuals, and institutions use card records.

Since acceptable filing procedures must be followed and reliable systems must be used if records are to be of maximum utility, it is important that those who establish and operate card systems be familiar with the principles of card filing.

Nature of Card Record Systems There are many different types of card files. In Chapter 1 a card file for names and addresses was described. In Chapter 10 an alphabetic card index file as a supplement to a numeric correspondence file was discussed. It is the purpose of this chapter to describe several other types of card file systems.

Card records may be filed vertically or horizontally. In the vertical method cards are placed on edge, and vertical guides are used to mark sections in the file drawer in a manner similar to that used in all types of correspondence files. In the horizontal method cards are placed flat, in overlapping positions, usually in long, shallow trays that can be stored in cabinets. The overlapping of the cards makes the lower edge of each card visible when the tray is pulled from the cabinet. For this reason, and for others which will be explained later, horizontal card files are called "card visible files" or, more commonly, "visible files."

Because the equipment and the guiding systems for vertical and visible card files are so dissimilar, each type will be given separate consideration in this chapter.

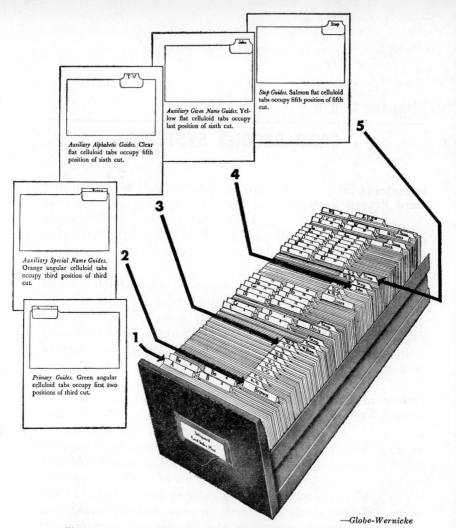

Auxiliary Alphabetic Guides. Clear flat celluloid tabs occupy fifth position of sixth cut.

Auxiliary Given Name Guides. Yellow flat celluloid tabs occupy last position of sixth cut.

Stop Guides. Salmon flat celluloid tabs occupy fifth position of fifth cut.

Auxiliary Special Name Guides. Orange angular celluloid tabs occupy third position of third cut.

Primary Guides. Green angular celluloid tabs occupy first two positions of third cut.

—*Globe-Wernicke*

Illustration 14A, Alphabetic Guiding System for Name File

Vertical Card Files

Systems of Vertical Card Files Any of the commonly used systems—alphabetic, numeric, geographic, and subject—can be used for a vertical card file. Both alphabetic and geographic systems can be used for card records concerning sales information and/or data about customers, depending upon the relative importance of personal names or geographical locations to the operation of a particular business.

Illustration 14A shows an alphabetic system for a name vertical card file. Notice that primary guides divide the cards alphabetically, secondary guides designate commonly found names, third position guides break the name sections into subdivisions, and fourth position guides further break down the name sections and also show the end of each alphabetic section in the file.

A typical example of the use of a subject system for card records is the usual method of keeping stock records. The subject method is used as the guiding system for stock records because each card in such a file carries a history of one item in stock. The important factor in filing and finding a stock record card is knowing the subject title (name) of the stock item and/or the name of the group of items of which the item is a part. Illustration 14B shows a guiding system that might serve in a stock record file. Guide notations for stock and inventory card files frequently show subject titles followed by some form of numeric notations (stock numbers).

Illustration 14B, Subject Card File

—*Yawman and Erbe*

Signals for Vertical Card Files Finding the different types of information or data included on card records in a vertical file is facilitated by the use of one or more of the following types of signals.

1. If the guides have hollow tabs, the notation may be typed on different colored slips so that each color will indicate a different type of information.

2. Cards of different colors can be used. For example, in a personnel file cards of one color can be used for men and those of another color for women. Also, a manufacturing business that sells to both wholesalers and retailers might use cards of one color for wholesalers and cards of a second color for retailers.

3. Some cards have special code symbols printed across the top edge. The file clerk selects the proper code for the information on the card and cuts from the top edge of the card all of the other codes, so that the one selected is left as a signal tab.

4. Small colored movable signals may be attached to the tops of the file cards so that the position as well as the color classifies the information on the card. In a credit file, for example, a red signal could be attached to a particular position on a card to indicate that an account was one month overdue. A black signal could be attached in another position to indicate that an account was two months overdue. In this manner a credit manager could tell at a glance the number of delinquent accounts and the age of each account. Furthermore, credit references could be made much more easily than would be possible if each card had to be pulled from the file and read in detail to secure the desired information.

Special Indexing Systems In addition to the four major filing systems, methods using color and sound have been introduced into vertical card files.

Color is used in the adaptation of the Variadex system (described on pages 69 and 70) for card filing purposes. The card system is identical in plan with that used for correspondence filing except that only guide tabs are used in the card file.

The factor of sound has been developed for card systems by a method called Soundex. The Soundex system is described in detail later in this chapter.

Visible Card Files

**Methods of
Handling Visible
Records**

As previously mentioned, cards in a visible file are usually held horizontally in trays, but there are three additional ways of keeping visible records. Cards (or sheets) may be held in overlapping positions in loose-leaf books. They may also be held in a vertical position with each card cut so that its upper right-hand corner is visible. Because such cards are held in very wide tubs, five or more cards can be set in staggered positions across the width of the tub so that the side edge of each card is always visible.

In the fourth method of handling visible records, rotary units are attached to a central post (somewhat in the manner of book leaves) around which the panels may be swung into position. Rotary units may be in the form of celluloid pockets to hold cards in overlapping sections, or they may be con‐ structed to hold portions of cards showing only one or two lines of typewritten information.

In technical terminology these four visible methods are known as (1) card visible files, (2) loose-leaf visible books, (3) vertical-visible files, and (4) reference visible files.

**Systems for Card
Visible Files**

In card visible files the primary guiding notations appear on labels which are in‐ serted into holders on the outside of each drawer or tray in a cabinet. Captions on these labels show the range of the group of cards held in each tray.

Inside the tray the visible edge of each card shows an identifying mark which assists in finding cards and keeping them in an orderly arrangement. The mark of identification will correspond to the major system used in a particular file, whether it is alphabetic, numeric, geographic, subject, or a combination of these.

In Illustration 14C, notice that outside labels show that this card visible file is in the sales department and that the open tray holds sales record cards for firms whose names fall in the alphabetic division A to H. Notice also that cards in the open drawer have been separated so that the whole face of

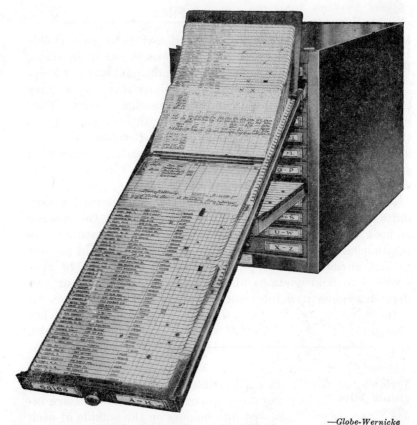

—*Globe-Wernicke*

Illustration 14C, Card Visible Cabinet

one particular card is visible. Cards below the division show firm names and signal markings on the visible edges. Cards above the division also show names and signal markings so that any card in the tray can be located regardless of the position of other cards above or below it.

The primary guiding system for card visible files may be varied to meet the particular requirements for a given file. The secondary guiding system, which appears on the visible edge of each card, is equally flexible. Personal names, subjects, city names, dates, or decimal or serial numbers can be shown singly or in combination as secondary notations on the visible edge of the cards.

Signal Systems for One of the most useful and distinctive
Visible Records   features of visible records is that they
can be signaled (marked) to show a
great variety of summary information. When visible cards
are so signaled, many vital facts can be determined without
recourse to a detailed examination of the data on a whole
card or a series of cards. Signal marks can be made on the
cards by hand, or signal devices can be selected from a variety
of types manufactured of metal or plastic materials.

Signals can be used to show such information as the amount
of stock on hand at any given time (stock record cards), the
volume of sales or the percentage of quota on sales (sales
record cards), the number of overdue accounts and the length
of time each is overdue (credit and collection cards), and the
date for follow-up on any matter concerning accounts, con-
tacts, etc.

Signal marks are shown in Illustration 14C on the right-
hand side of the cards in the open tray. In Illustration 14D,
colored, movable signals show important data for sales control. Signals on the left side of the visible edge of each card
show the last month that a sale was made to each company.

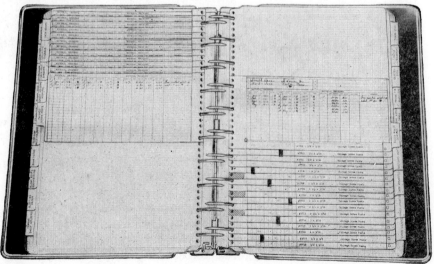

—*Wilson-Jones Company*

Illustration 14D, Signal Marks on Visible Records

**Loose-Leaf
Visible Systems**
Loose-leaf cards or sheets that are held in prong binders or ring binders are widely used where voluminous data must be kept in a relatively small space. An advantage of this system is that the binders are portable.

Loose-leaf visible cards are available in several forms. Some binders hold cards so that bottom edges are visible. Others hold them so that top edges show, while still others are arranged so that the side edges are visible.

The types of records kept in loose-leaf form are as varied as those kept in card visible files. They include cards for records of stock, data on purchasing, accounting or record-keeping data, and many other types of records.

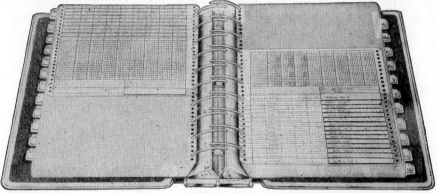

—Wilson-Jones Company

Illustration 14E, Loose-Leaf Binder

**Vertical-Visible
Files**
Vertical-visible files are a rather recent development in the field of filing. Essentially, this type of filing is a combination of vertical and visible because cards are filed in vertical position (on edge) but are cut and positioned so that each card has one or two visible edges.

One visible edge is formed by a diagonal cut across the upper corner of each card. A second visible edge results from these cards being held in very wide tub frames that allow 5 to 10 cards to be staggered across the width of the tub to form one row so that the edge of each card can be seen.

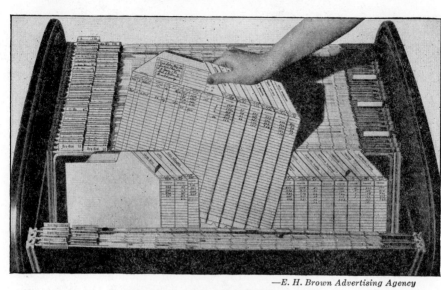

—*E. H. Brown Advertising Agency*
Illustration 14F, Vertical-Visible Tub

As shown in Illustration 14F, the guides used in vertical-visible files are similar to those used in vertical correspondence or card files and may follow any of the major systems.

Although vertical-visible files are most commonly used for accounting and bookkeeping records, especially when they are posted by machine, they can be used to hold any of the types of records previously mentioned.

Transparent Tube Equipment Many active business records require only a name, or a name, and an address, or a name and a code number. Obviously a whole card would not be needed for the keeping of such a record. Transparent tube equipment is generally used for keeping such records. This equipment consists of sections of visible trays or frames made to hold narrow insert slips. A name, or other required information, is typed on these slips, which are then inserted into the tubes of the visible frame.

A few of the uses for this type of equipment are: customers' indexes, credit rating records, mailing lists, cross indexes, pricing records, and telephone switchboard indexes.

—*E. H. Brown Advertising Agency*

Illustration 14G, Transparent Tube File

Wheel Files Modern card equipment includes the use of wheel files. One type is known as the Wheeldex File, in which a wheel stands upright, revolving about a horizontal axle. Cards are punched at the bottom to slip over a metal rod surrounding the wheel and are filed in upright position.

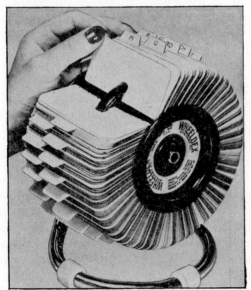

The cards ride securely and can be inserted or removed with ease. The wheels can be mounted in suitable desks or cabinets, and any card may be located quickly by rotating the wheel.

—*Wheeldex Manufacturing Company*

Illustration 14H,
A Wheel File

Principle of Sound in Card Files

Soundex The Soundex System is designed to bring all names
System   that sound the same but are spelled differently into
             one section of a card index file. Such names as
Berke, Birk, and Burke, which would be placed in different
sections of an ordinary alphabetic file, are brought together
in a file of this kind.

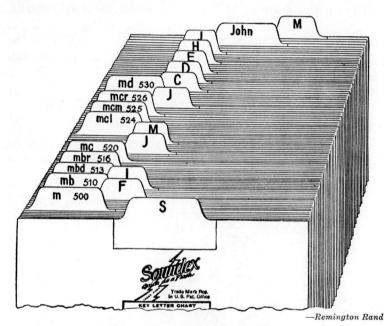

—*Remington Rand*

Illustration 141, Soundex Index

An advantage of this system of filing is that it prevents
duplication of names that might result from different spellings
of the same name or from a change in the spelling of a name.
When a name is taken from a signature on a letter or a form,
it does not matter in this system if the "i's" and "e's" cannot
be distinguished because both are disregarded in determining
the code symbol; nor does it matter if "n's" and "m's" cannot
be distinguished because "m," according to this system, stands
for "n" as well as for itself.

Another advantage of this system is that of simplifying the file clerk's work when a request for certain papers is communicated by telephone. The file clerk does not need to know the correct spelling of the name in order to locate rather rapidly the material requested if all names that are pronounced alike are filed in the same section.

The Soundex card index is most useful for large name files. The federal government, for example, uses the system for classifying the millions of names on social security records.

Coding   In the Soundex System each name is coded on the basis of its first filing or indexing unit in the following manner:

1. The first part of the code consists of a capital letter that is identical with the first letter of the first filing unit of the name. (Consonants and vowels alike are considered.)
2. The numeric part of the code symbol consists of three figures; it is based upon certain key letters that stand for the second and succeeding letters of the first filing unit in the name.
3. In determining the numeric part of the code symbol, the vowels, a, e, i, o, and u, and the consonants w, h, and y are disregarded. All other consonants are assigned code figures, which are based on the following table:

KEY LETTER	LETTERS REPRESENTED BY KEY LETTER	CODE FIGURE
b	b, f, p, v	1
c	c, g, j, k, q, s, x, z	2
d	d, t	3
l	l	4
m	m, n	5
r	r	6

As an example, the name "Smith" is coded S-530. The letters in the name "Smith" are considered in this manner: S, as the first letter of the name, becomes the first part of the code; m is its own key letter and is represented by "5"; i is a vowel and is disregarded; t is represented by the key letter "d" and the code figure "3"; h is a disregarded consonant. Since all code numbers in this system must consist of three figures, the cipher "0" is added. The resulting code for the name "Smith" is S-530.

"Smythe" would also be coded S-530. The *y, h,* and *e* letters would be disregarded. A name like "See," which contains no key letters, is coded S-000 and is filed directly behind the primary "S" guide.

4. When two or more consecutive letters have the same key letter, only the first of such letters is considered.

```
Name—            Stock
Key Letters—     Sd c   (Disregard o and k)
Code—            S3 2    0 —written S-320
```

5. When a key letter or its equivalent immediately follows an initial letter of the same value, the second letter is not coded.

```
Name—            School
Key Letters—     S  1   (Disregard c, h, and o)
Code—            S  4    0 0 —written S-400
```

6. When two letters having the same key letter are separated by "h" or "w," the third letter in the group is not considered.

```
Name—            Boughs
Key Letters—     B   c   (Disregard o, u, h, and s)
Code—            B   2    0 0 —written B-200
```

7. When two letters having the same key letter value are separated by a vowel or the letter "y," the third letter in the group is considered.

```
Name—            Statler
Key Letters—     Sd   dl
Code—            S3   34     —written S-334
```

Guides   The guides that are used in the Soundex Card Index File and which are shown in Illustration 14I, page 149, are of the following types:

1. The primary guides in center position refer to the first letters of the first filing units of names of persons, businesses, and organizations. These primary guides serve the purpose of dividing the file into major alphabetic sections.

2. First-position guides indicate the key letters and the code numbers of the second and succeeding letters in the first filing units of names.

3. Guides in second position with single letter captions are used to indicate the first letters of the second units in names.

4. Guides in other positions are used to subdivide the congested sections following certain guides in second position.

A card for David M. Smith would be filed in the S section (indicated by a middle-position primary guide) behind the "md-530" first-position guide and behind the "D" second-position guide. A card for The Schmokel Foundries would be filed in the S section behind the "mcl-524" first-position guide.

The arrangement of cards behind any one guide is alphabetic according to the second indexing unit if the second units are not alike in the names concerned. If the second indexing units are alike, the third must be considered. In other words, the regular rules for alphabetic indexing apply to all units except the first.

QUESTIONS

1. What are some of the advantages of keeping cards in a file rather than a list of names and addresses in a book?

2. Why are card records sometimes called secondary records?

3. Give several advantages of the use of the Soundex System of filing cards.

4. How is the first part of the code for a name determined in the Soundex System of coding?

5. Of how many symbols does the numeric part of the code consist?

6. Which vowels and consonants are disregarded in the Soundex System?

7. What is the purpose of the primary guides in center position in a Soundex Card Index File?

8. What are the purposes of the guides in the other positions in this type of file?

9. What type of information is given on personnel cards?

10. What type of information must employers keep for social security records?

11. What is a visible card file?

12. What is a visible rotary unit?

13. For what kinds of information is transparent tube equipment used?

14. Give examples of the ways in which signals may be used in card files.

15. How are signals for visible card files used?

PROBLEMS

1. (a) Type or write each of the following names on a 5″ x 3″ card in index order. (b) Code each name according to the rules of the Soundex System and write the code number on the card. The card for Item 1 would be arranged as follows:

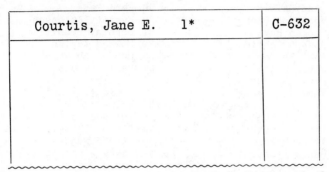

| Courtis, Jane E. 1* | C-632 |

* The number on the card is the number of the first name in the list. It is used here for ease in checking the solution to the problem.

(c) Arrange the cards in filing order.

1. Courtis, Jane E.
2. Reed, Harold
3. Cannon, Norman
4. Peirs, Rufus
5. Bair, Paul
6. Kuhn, Charles
7. Cramer Convalescent Home
8. Bier, Walter F.
9. Canan, Louise
10. Pearce, Rutherford
11. Cameron, William
12. Peyton, Lloyd
13. Curtis, Anna M.
14. Luecke, Richard
15. Fay, John L.
16. Kammerer, Arthur
17. Read, James
18. Kahr, Julia
19. Luke, Paul
20. Pierse, Charles
21. Beyer, Irene
22. Fife, Marie
23. Foye, Elmer
24. Ade, Robert
25. Bayer, Walter G.
26. Phyfe, Ellen
27. Frey, Arthur
28. Schramm, William
29. Curtiss, Dorothy R.
30. Coon, Edward
31. Kramer, Melvin
32. Baer, George W.
33. Eade, Albert
34. Canon, Harold
35. Carr, Webster
36. Pierce, Roland
37. Shram, Oscar
38. Koon, David G.
39. Cannan, Mary
40. Reid, Fred
41. Behr, Gus
42. Schram, Ray
43. Karr, John
44. Faye, Robert
45. Look, William
46. Payton, Thomas
47. Aide, Lena
48. Kraymer, Anthony
49. Foy, Irvin
50. Fey, John E.

2. (a) Type or write each of the following names on a 5″ x 3″ card in index order. (b) Code each name according to the rules of the Soundex System and write the code number on the card. (c) Arrange the cards in filing order.

1. John Bauer
2. Timothy Boughser
3. Carol Schaeffer
4. Linn Gaines
5. Mortimer Bier
6. Thomas Hamond
7. Joseph Schmidt
8. Paul Rhodes
9. Elvin Aldrich
10. Paula Rhoads
11. Paul McCune
12. Milburn Adreon
13. James M. Daley
14. Carrie Bayne
15. Allen Rogers
16. Henry Albrecht
17. Fred McKune
18. Orin Patterson
19. Alan Beer
20. Michael Boughcer
21. Charles Schafer
22. Verne Fort
23. Amos Rodgers
24. Paul A. McMillin
25. Charles Dailey

26. Gustave Bain
27. Ronald Beier
28. James T. Daly
29. Earl Bane
30. Everett Paterson
31. Dorothy Schmit
32. Howard Adrian
33. Hubert Boughzer
34. Paul Hammond
35. Pauline Roads
36. David Aldridge
37. Velma Pfort
38. Yolanda Harte
39. Clyde Schmitt
40. Otto Bower
41. Joyce Albright
42. Doris Daily
43. Wallace Hart
44. Donald Shafer
45. William Heart
46. Virginia Forte
47. Paul L. McMillan
48. Edward Schaffer
49. Adam Beere
50. Lillian Gaynes

JOB 10—SOUNDEX CODING PRACTICE

At this time complete Job 10 in FILING OFFICE PRAC-TICE, Second Edition. The instructions and supplies for this job are included in the practice set.

Chapter • 15

○ ESTABLISHING AND MAINTAINING
• FILING SYSTEMS

Individual A filing system suited to individual office
Filing Systems requirements can be planned by a person who
is familiar with filing principles and prac-
tices, available equipment and supplies, and the filing problems
that are peculiar to the business. In planning such a system,
or in making improvements in an existing system, a person
should consider the factors indicated by the following ques-
tions.

1. What types of materials other than correspondence need
   to be filed?
2. What volume of each type of material needs to be handled
   each year or every six months?
3. What is the nature of the materials? Are they suited
   to a direct alphabetic, numeric, subject, or geographic
   system, or some combination of these?
4. What kind of charge and follow-up method will be most
   satisfactory?
5. How frequently should materials be transferred? What
   method of transfer will attain the greatest efficiency in
   the use of time, available floor space, and equipment?
6. What types of card-record forms and card files will be
   needed?
7. To what extent can the existing filing equipment, if any,
   be utilized?
8. What departmental files will be maintained in addition to
   the central filing department?

Central and Those companies which establish a cen-
Departmental Files tral filing department experience the
fewest difficulties with their record-keep-
ing. The advantages of centralization are that it:

1. Places responsibility on one file supervisor,
2. Eliminates duplication of records,
3. Provides for better quality of work and greater speed,
4. Provides for wider use of filing equipment,
5. Permits standarization of filing equipment.
6. Saves time in locating material.

In very large companies, where one central filing department is ruled out because it is impossible to locate it centrally, files are established by floors, with a central file serving all the departments on a floor.

Illustration 15A, Centralized Filing Department

Usually a central file houses all general materials, as well as copies of certain records and reports which are primarily of a departmental nature. The original copies of such papers are stored in departmental files. This arrangement makes all materials of general interest available to all departments, and yet allows each department to retain papers vital to departmental operations. Operating departments usually keep their own personnel records, credit material, and purchasing catalogs, and their working tools, such as tax services, engineering data, and catalogs.

The files for the executive and purchasing departments of a corporation are quite typical of departmental files. The executive department files may hold such materials as corporate reports, minutes of meetings of stockholders and the board of directors, stock and bond reports, appraisals, audits, and financial statements. The files in the purchasing department may house catalogs, price lists, requisitions, purchase orders, stock and inventory records, and certain correspondence that is not released to the central filing department until current transactions are completed.

Filing Cabinets   After a careful analysis of the filing needs of a business has been made and a plan for filing operations has been outlined, the next step is the selection of the proper equipment and supplies—cabinets, guides, and folders.

Correspondence cabinets are available in units of from one to five drawers in height. Correspondence files, three drawers in height, are often used as counters; for this reason they are called "counter height files." Cabinets for other kinds of materials are built to this convenient height also. Four-drawer and five-drawer correspondence cabinets are very often used as partitions between departments or sections of an office.

Cabinets are made with these sections: legal, check, document, invoice, insurance, map and plan, and card. Combination units made up of letter and card sections or card and check sections are available. Substitute drawers, which may be ordered separately, can be put into cabinets in the place of the original drawers. For example, two check drawers or two card drawers can be inserted into the space formerly taken by one correspondence drawer.

Heavy cabinets or safe files are made to house valuable papers. Specially constructed cabinets, insulated for protection against fire damage, are also available on the market. Note the card, check, document, and correspondence file on page 158.

Cabinet   Since cabinet dimensions vary, capacities of file
Capacities   drawers also vary slightly because of differences in drawer length. The average correspondence file drawer will house an approximate maximum of 5,000 items in addition to the necessary guides and folders. The

—*Globe-Wernicke*

Illustration 15B, Card, Check, Document, and Correspondence
Sections on a Truck Base

files can be used much more efficiently, however, if the number of pieces in each drawer is kept below the maximum. As
the maximum capacity is approached, another drawer should
be added. When a drawer is only partially filled, a piece of
metal or wood in the back, called a *follower*, is fixed in such
a position that it keeps the materials in an upright position.

Card file cabinets are made in a variety of sizes. Units may
be purchased to house any number of cards. Small cards trays
hold from 100 to 500 cards, while cabinets hold as many as
90,000. A twenty-eight inch drawer will hold approximately
3,880 cards.

Cabinets are made with drawers of different sizes to house
cards of various sizes. The most commonly used cards are
those of sizes 5″ x 3″, 6″ x 4″, and 8″ x 5″.

Guides   After a decision has been made concerning the kinds of cabinets needed, guides must be selected in the proper amount. Whether the filing system is to be made up in the office, or ordered as a completely equipped unit, it is important not to order too many or too few guides.

The Oxford Filing Supply Company suggests the following number of guides per drawer for correspondence and card files:

Alphabetic Index Required	Drawers of Correspondence	Number of Cards
25 divisions (A–Z)	1	Up to 500 cards
40 divisions (A–Z)	2	500– 800 cards
80 divisions (A–Z)	3– 4	800– 1,600 cards
120 divisions (A–Z)	5– 6	1,600– 2,400 cards
160 divisions (A–Z)	7– 8	2,400– 3,200 cards
240 divisions (A–Z)	9–12	3,200– 4,800 cards
320 divisions (A–Z)	13–16	4,800– 6,500 cards
480 divisions (A–Z)	17–24	6,500–10,000 cards
720 divisions (A–Z)	25–36	10,000–15,000 cards
1,000 divisions (A–Z)	37–50	15,000–20,000 cards

To attain best results with card files, not more than twenty cards should be filed behind one guide. If cards in one section exceed this number, a new guide should be added to divide the section.

Guides for card files are cut to several standard tab widths. The most common of these are one-fifth cut, one-third cut, and one-half cut. They are available with blank tabs or with printed alphabetic, numeric, geographic, subject, and date notations.

Card guides with special index notations are made by most filing supply manufacturers. A commercial card index frequently is an adaptation of the special correspondence alphabetic index manufactured by the same company. For example, there is a Triple Check Automatic Index, manufactured by Remington Rand, Inc., for card files as well as for correspondence files; and there is a Safeguard Index, manufactured by the Globe-Wernicke Company, for both card and correspondence files.

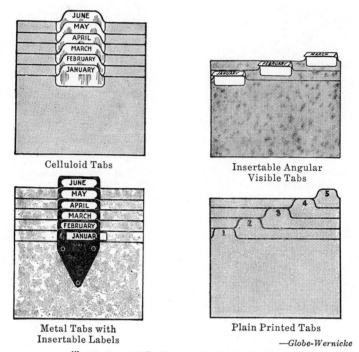

Celluloid Tabs

Insertable Angular
Visible Tabs

Metal Tabs with
Insertable Labels

Plain Printed Tabs

—*Globe-Wernicke*

Illustration 15C, Types of Card Guides

Folders   For quick reference, not more than seven folders should be put behind one guide. An exception is made in some numeric files because numeric folder captions are so easy to read and because it is convenient to number guides in multiples of ten, such as 300, 310, 320.

Usually a folder should not hold more than thirty pieces of correspondence or similar material. With more than this number of pieces, filing and finding are difficult and time-consuming.

When an individual folder becomes crowded, it can be subdivided by time periods. If the transfer period is one year, one individual folder could be reserved for January-June materials and another with the same correspondent for July-December materials. For very active correspondents a separate folder could be used for the materials of each month.

When a miscellaneous folder becomes crowded, the number of such folders in the drawer should be increased so that each will include materials for a smaller alphabetic range. For example, if the one "A" miscellaneous folder becomes too full, a miscellaneous folder and guide for "An" could be added.

Notations for Tabs and Labels If an individual filing system is constructed, it is not enough to know how many guides are needed. The person responsible for organizing, revising, or expanding the filing system must know also what captions to use on insert slips or gummed labels for guide and miscellaneous alphabetic folder tabs.

The desirable breakdown or division of the alphabet for alphabetic files has been studied by a number of filing manufacturers. The Yawman and Erbe Company has found that, out of a thousand names, six letters occurred as the first letter of the first filing unit 510 times. S occurred 108 times; B, 93; M, 88; H, 78; C, 74; and W, 69. As a result of studies of this kind, the captions for 40, 80, 120, or 160 guides in a file can be such that the materials will be quite uniformly distributed throughout the alphabetic sections. For example, the Oxford Filing Supply Company lists the following A and B captions for a 40-division index (40 guides): A, B, Bi, Br. For an 80-division index, these capitions are expanded to the following list: A, An, B, Be, Bi, Bo, Bra, Bro, Bu. In a 120-division index, the A captions become A, Al, An, As and there are 11 B captions. For 160 divisions, there are six A captions and 15 B captions. In any number of divisions, there should be more captions for S than for any other letter because S is the most frequent initial letter of first indexing units of names. While this breakdown of the alphabet is applicable for the nation as a whole, it may vary in some localities and areas, especially where a given nationality background is common to a large group of the population.

Signal Systems Correspondence filing is facilitated by (1) reserving each tab position for one type of guide or folder, (2) using numbers in addition to letters and words for guide and folder captions, and (3) using colored tabs.

When insert slips or gummed labels are used on tabs and are typed in the office, several ways of making color signals can be used. One way consists of alternating red and black typing background for captions on tabs in the several positions across the file drawer. A second way is to use different colored insert slips or labels for the different positions. Similar results are achieved by using transparent celluloid strips of different colors that can be inserted in front of guide and/or folder tabs.

Miscellaneous Equipment and Supplies   For maximum efficiency, a filing department should provide sorting equipment, file stools, file trays, and thumbers for its clerks. Sorters are essential. A familiar sorter is an open tray with low sides, equipped with strong guides, but growing in popularity is the sorting device that lies flat on the desk and which has hinged guides under which papers are placed while sorting. Some of these devices operate on a track and can be moved from left to right and vice versa so that the desired letter or number is brought to a position that is in front of or beside the sorting clerk.

Keeping Files in Good Order   Most important to efficient filing and finding is keeping the files in good order. Too often files are well planned and managed when they are newly assembled, but because of careless filing and lack of organization, they soon become overcrowded and generally "run down."

Here are a few points to watch in keeping files well organized, neat, and useful:

1. There should be a definitely planned filing routine.
    a. Even though filing is only a part of general office routine in a small office, a definite allotment of time should be made for filing and keeping files in order. Orderly and efficient filing systems cannot be expected when work is neglected or allowed to accumulate.

b. Definite indexing and alphabetizing rules should always be followed.

c. Someone should be given responsibility of directing filing procedure and making final decisions regarding filing problems.

d. Only personnel assigned to filing should place papers in folders or refile folders.

e. A manual of procedure should be prepared and kept up-to-date by the file supervisor. This provides an excellent training tool, as well as serving as a reference for any question that may arise as to the standard procedure for an operation.

2. Folders and drawers should not be crowded, and filing should always be an orderly process.

a. Folders, sections, drawers, and cabinets should be added as file material increases. Room should be allowed in file drawers and throughout the whole filing system for expansion. The file should not be crowded when it is installed.

b. A definite transfer schedule should be planned in order to relieve drawers and folders of inactive material.

c. There should not be too many folders behind one guide, or too many cards behind one guide.

d. Cabinets with followers or some kind of compression type of drawer should be used to keep folders from sagging.

e. File drawers should always be properly labeled on the front to indicate their contents.

f. An "overnight drawer" should be provided so that at the end of a working day desks can be cleared of papers and materials which are to be processed the next day. In this way "to be processed" materials can be found in one place.

3. Worn folders should be replaced at definite intervals of time.

4. Papers should be placed neatly in folders, not crammed in, with edges folded back. Torn papers should be mended.

5. Pins and clips should never be left on papers when they are filed. Pins are dangerous, and clips are bulky and have a tendency to catch on other papers.

6. The tops of file cabinets should be kept clear of material.

QUESTIONS

1. Name several factors that must be considered when an individual filing system is planned.
2. Can a central filing department and a departmental file be used in the same company?
3. Give examples of items that are filed in executive department files.
4. What units of drawers are available in correspondence cabinets?
5. What are counter height files?
6. What kinds of correspondence cabinets are often used as partitions between departments or sections of an office?
7. Give examples of the various kinds of forms that are filed in sections of filing cabinets.
8. How many items, in addition to the necessary guides and folders, will the average correspondence file drawer house?
9. What is a follower in a file drawer?
10. What are the most common sizes of cards filed in card files?
11. What is the maximum number of cards that should be filed behind one guide if best results are to be attained?
12. What are the most common tab widths of guides for card files?
13. What is the maximum number of folders that should be put behind each guide for quick reference?
14. How many pieces of correspondence or similar material can a folder hold comfortably?
15. When an individual folder becomes crowded, how can it be subdivided?
16. For what letter of the alphabet should there be the most captions in an alphabetic file? Why?
17. How are colored tabs used in the files?
18. Give several points to be followed in keeping the files well organized, neat, and useful.

PROBLEMS

1. The following information pertains to the sales department of a wholesale candy company that is located at Hammond, Indiana.

    a. The business is limited to six states: Illinois, Indiana, Iowa, Michigan, Ohio, and Wisconsin.

b. There is one salesman assigned to each state and, in addition, one for each of the following cities: Chicago, Des Moines, Detroit, Indianapolis, and Springfield (Ill.).

c. All orders are filed at Hammond. All correspondence concerning orders is kept in the sales department files.

d. There is a limited number of active customer correspondents. There is considerable general correspondence with customers in Chicago and Detroit.

How should the sales department files of this company be organized? Include in your answer the following points:

a. Should the system be alphabetic, numeric, geographic, or subject?
b. What captions should be used on the primary guide tabs?
c. What auxiliary guides should be used?
d. What kinds of folders should be used?

2. The Westfield Office Equipment Company wholesales many kinds of filing equipment to retail dealers. The following is an outline of only a few of the items that are carried in stock:

200 Series—Transfer Cases
Single Drawer—letter size
Single Drawer—ledger size
Single Drawer—check size

300 Series—Vertical Filing Cabinets
Two Drawer—letter size
Two Drawer—letter size—with lock
Three Drawer—letter size
Three Drawer—letter size—with roller bearings
Four Drawer—letter size

400 Series—Card Cabinets
Twelve Drawer—5" x 3"
Ten Drawer—5" x 3"
Nine Drawer—3¼" x 2½"
Six Drawer—8" x 5"

Prepare a chart of the arrangement of guides and cards for a stock record card file, using the items in the outline. Use numeric captions only. Then prepare an outline showing the subjects or articles for which the numeric captions stand.

3. An independent retail store of average size has correspondence that totals 8,000 pieces per year with manufacturers, wholesalers, and customers. About half of the sales are on a credit basis.

a. If the transfer period is a year, how large a correspondence file cabinet (how many drawers) is needed?
b. Should the correspondence file be alphabetic, numeric, subject, or geographic?
c. If an alphabetic system is used for correspondence, how many primary guides are needed—40, 80, or 120?
d. For what purposes could card files be used? What kind of card file would be best in each case?
e. For what purposes could signals be used in the card systems?

4. The publisher of a national monthly magazine receives new and renewal subscriptions throughout the year. Before a subscription expires, the subscriber is notified. When a subscription is not renewed, the subscriber's name is removed from the active files.

a. If the primary guides of a card file for subscribers bear date (month) captions, what captions could be used for auxiliary or secondary guides?
b. What items of information should be included on each subscriber's card?
c. Should signals be used on the subscription cards? If so, for what purposes?
d. How should subscription cards for more than one year be filed?
e. What provision for transfer should be made?

INDEX

A

Abbreviations, in firm names, 19; in names of individuals, 12

Accession Book or Register, 98

Addresses, of businesses, 23; of individuals, 14; use of word "City" in, 14, 23

Alpha-Numeric filing system, 119, 120

Alphabetic card file, 6; illustration of, 7; *See* Card files

Alphabetic catalog filing, 135

Alphabetic correspondence file, arrangement of guides and folders, 42, 46, 64; drawer of an, 43; file section with special name guide, 47; folders in an, 41; guides in an, 42; organization of, 40; special date sections, 48; special sections, 46; vertical filing, 40

Alphabetic correspondence filing procedure, 51; coding, rules and methods, 53, 54; cross referencing, 55; inspection, 53; release mark, 51, 52; sorting, 58; time stamps, 51

Alphabetic correspondence folders, 40, 41

Alphabetic correspondence guides, 42

Alphabetic file, miscellaneous, in a numeric file, 97, 98

Alphabetic guides, 6; tabs, 6; captions, 6; one-third-cut tabs, 6

Alphabetic guiding system, for name file, 140

Alphabetic indexing, definition of, 9; need of rules for, 8

Alphabetic subdivisions, 161

Apostrophe s ('s), 22

Applications, coding of correspondence pertaining to, 44-45, 54

Armed Forces decimal filing, 118

Articles, (English), disregard in indexing, 19; rule for filing title containing "The," 19

Articles, foreign, 20

Auxiliary card index in stencil filing, 137, 138

Auxiliary correspondence guides, 42

Auxiliary guides, in an alphabetic file, 42; in a

geographic file, 123-125; in a numeric file, 97; in a subject file, 108-109

B

Banks, indexing names of, 27

Blueprints, filing of, 136

Book type file, 40

Branches of one firm, filing correspondence with, 55

C

Cabinets, filing, *See* Filing cabinets

Captions, alphabetic, 41; closed, 64; combinations of letters and numbers in, 6, 41; double, 64; geographic, 123, 125; multiple closed, 65; numeric, 95; of folders, 40; single, 64; subject, 108-109

Captions on card guides, 6; combination of letters and numbers in, 6

Carbon copies of letters, color of, 36; as follow-up method, 87

Card File, Subject, 141

Card file cabinets, capacities of, 158; number of guides needed for, 159; sizes of, 158

Card files, color in, 69-70; cross referencing in, 30; loose-leaf visible, 146; methods of handling, 143; signals for, 142; signal systems for, 145; systems of, 140; supplementary, in numeric files, 97; vertical, 140; vertical-visible, 146; visible, 143

Card filing, 6; cross referencing in, 30; file cards in, 6; guides in, 6

Card follow-up systems, 87

Card guides, 6; captions of, 6; combination of letters and numbers in captions of, 6; number of cards filed behind, 159; purpose of, 6; range of cards filed behind, 6, 7; tab width of, 6; tabs of, 6; types of, 160; with metal tabs, 6

Card index, for a geographic file, 128; for a numeric file, 97; for a subject file, 108-110

Card index file, supplementary, 97

Card systems, importance and nature of, 139; sound in, 149; vertical, 140-141

Card tickler file, 86; with one form of requisition, 83

Card trays, 158

Carrier folder, 83

Catalogs, 135; file card in a subject card index for, 135

Celluloid tabs, 160

Central files. 155

Charge methods, carrier folder, 83; follow-up file, 82; on-call cards, 85; out card, 84; out folder, 83; out guide, 82; out-sheet method, 85; pending, 82; requisition card, 81; substitution cards, 84; tickler files, 82

Check, card, document, and correspondence file, 158

Churches, indexing names of, 27

"City," use of, in addresses, 14, 23

Clippings, filing of, 136

Closed notations, 64

Clubs, indexing names of, 27

Coding, definition of, 53; in a geographic file, 126; in a subject file, 110, in Triple Check Automatic Index, 76; methods of, in alphabetic filing system, 54; numeric, 110; preliminary name coding in a numeric file, 98; rules for, in alphabetic filing, 53; in Soundex System, 150

Color, as signals in card files, 142; in signal systems, 145; of carbon copies of letters, 36; of incoming and outgoing items, 36

Combined surnames in firm names, 32

Commercial filing systems, 65; improvements in alphabetic filing methods, 65, 66

Compound surnames, 11

Conjunctions, disregarded in indexing, 19

Controlling index, for geographic and subject filing in an alphabetic system, 129-130

Correspondence, coding, in an alphabetic filing system, 53; coding, in a geographic file, 126; coding in a numeric file, 98; coding in a subject file, 98; coding of personal, 53; filed vertically like cards, 40; placing in folders in an alphabetic file, 59; types of, 36; types to be filed, 5

Correspondence files, incoming items 36; interoffice communications, 36; need for, 36; purposes of, 39, 42; outgoing items, 36

167